FAT QUARTER
BAGS & PURSES

25 projects to make from short lengths of fabric

Susie Johns

First published 2018 by
Guild of Master Craftsman Publications Ltd
Castle Place, 166 High Street, Lewes,
East Sussex, BN7 1XU, UK

ISBN 978 1 78494 419 3

A catalogue record for this book is available from the
British Library.

Publisher Jonathan Bailey
Production Manager Jim Bulley
Senior Project Editor Sara Harper
Editor Cath Senker
Managing Art Editor Gilda Pacitti
Design & Art Direction Wayne Blades
Photographer Neal Grundy
Step photography Susie Johns
Models Buster and Rocky
Picture credit Cover illustrations: Shutterstock/Ohn Mar

Colour origination by GMC Reprographics

Printed and bound in China

A note on measurements

The imperial measurements in these projects are
converted from metric. While every attempt has
been made to ensure that they are as accurate
as possible, some rounding up or down has been
inevitable. For this reason, it is always best to
stick to one system or the other throughout
a project: do not mix metric and imperial units.

CONTENTS

INTRODUCTION

Bags are necessary items for carrying our stuff around and for storing things at home. A bag needs to be practical and functional, but it helps if it looks good too. And if you enjoy sewing, it makes sense to sew your own bags and purses.

The bags and purses in this book are all relatively quick and straightforward to make, and none of them require any specialist skills or expensive materials and equipment. You don't need much in the way of fabric to make a bag, so fat quarters are an ideal place to start. What is a fat quarter? It's simply a clever way of cutting a yard or metre of traditional quilting cotton fabric into four pieces. If you were to cut a quarter of a yard or metre from a length of fabric, you would have a strip measuring 9in (23cm) by the width of the fabric, which is usually 44 or 45in (112 or 114cm). A fat quarter is cut in a different way: cut half a yard/metre of fabric, then cut this piece in half. This gives you a piece of fabric approximately 18 x 22in (46 x 56cm). This squarish shape is, for most projects, far more versatile, and buying fat quarters of fabric also makes it possible to buy four different fabrics for the same cost as a yard or metre of a single design.

Fat quarters are a good way of building up a collection of colours or themes for a project. If you're anything like me, you will find it hard to resist buying lovely fabrics when you come across them in shop, fairs and markets, even when you don't have a particular project in mind. Add these to the bits left over from sewing sessions and you end up with a stash of offcuts and remnants waiting to be used.

The 25 practical and stylish projects in this book will help you to make the most of these materials, and you can personalize your bag or purse by choosing your own combinations of colours and patterns. I hope you find these bags and purses as much fun to make as they are to use. I certainly enjoyed designing them! Whether you decide to make them for yourself or as gifts, the finished items are sure to attract admiring glances and plenty of compliments.

Susie

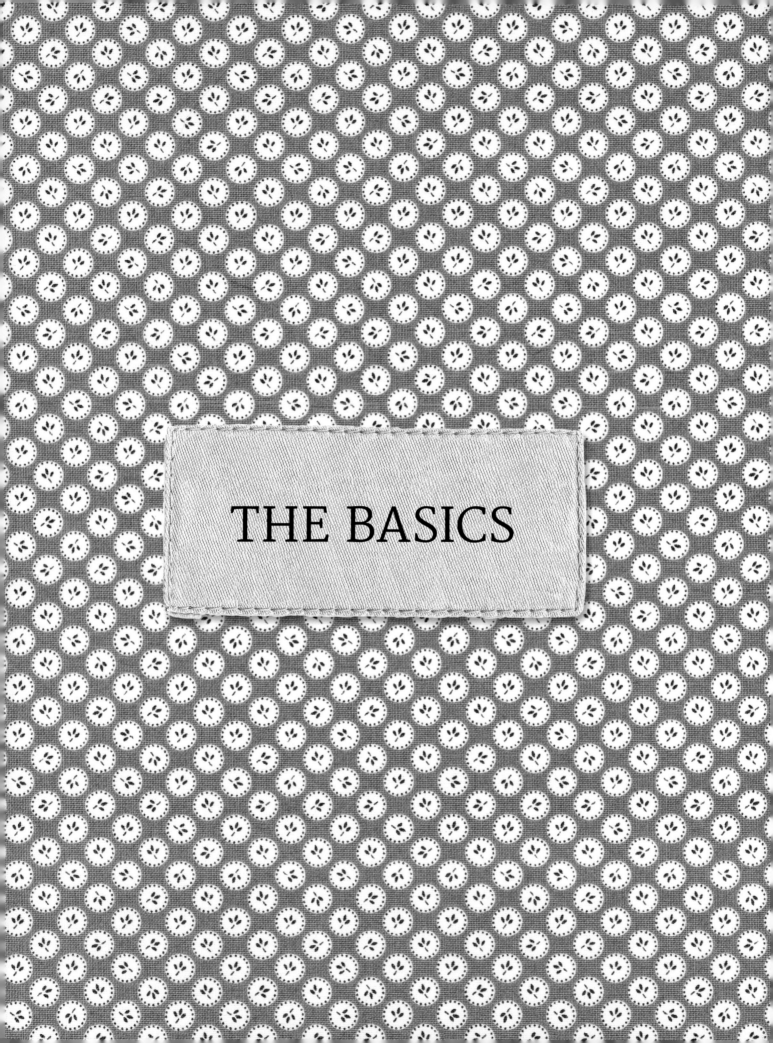

THE BASICS

MATERIALS & EQUIPMENT

If you are keen on sewing, the chances are you will already have most of the tools and equipment needed to complete the projects in this book. All you will have to buy are some fat quarters of fabrics in your choice of colours and designs.

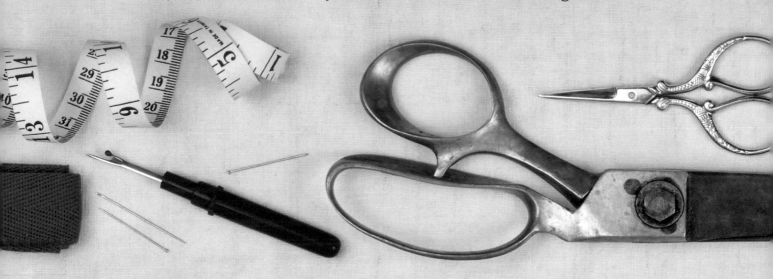

MEASURING You will need a long, flexible tape measure and a ruler for drawing lines on fabric. A set square or right-angled ruler helps to measure neat corners. Make sure you use imperial or metric measurements and do not mix the two.

SCISSORS You will need dressmaking scissors for cutting fabrics and small, pointed embroidery scissors for snipping threads. Pinking shears are also useful for trimming raw edges on seams, to prevent fraying. Use a separate pair of scissors for cutting paper, as this tends to blunt the blades.

SEAM RIPPER This tool is useful for cutting individual stitches and unpicking seams without damaging the fabric. Insert the pointed blade underneath the stitch to be cut, then push it forwards against the thread.

PINS Pinning and basting layers of fabric together prevents them from slipping when stitching so you can produce a straight seam. When machine stitching a seam, place pins at right angles. Pins with glass heads are easy to handle and to find. Sometimes, pins distort the fabric or are difficult to use when there are lots of layers, in which case you may find it easier to use binding clips, or small bulldog clips. Safety pins are useful for threading elastic and cords through casings.

NEEDLES Sharps are an all-rounder for hand sewing, with a round eye that is easy to thread. For embroidery, an embroidery (crewel) needle has a longer eye, to accommodate thicker thread.

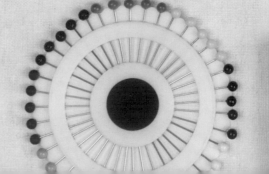

THREADS Use cotton thread when sewing cotton fabrics. It is made in a wide range of colours. For neatness, choose a thread to match the background colour of the fabric; when an exact match is not available, choose a shade slightly darker rather than lighter. For decorative stitching, embroidery thread is more substantial than ordinary sewing thread. Place the fabric to be stitched in an embroidery hoop, which holds it taut while you sew.

BOBBINS Keep a small stock of bobbins loaded with different coloured threads, and ready for use. When combining different-coloured fabrics, it can be useful to use one colour as the top thread and a different colour on the bobbin.

IRON You should press fabric before measuring and cutting, then press the work regularly when sewing, for a neat, professional finish. A good steam iron is essential. Your ironing board should be firm and stable, with a well-padded surface.

FABRICS Cotton fabrics are widely available as pre-cut fat quarters. These have been used throughout this book as the main fabrics for the outer part of each bag or purse, and in most cases for the lining as well. Other lining materials include clear vinyl, ripstop nylon and silk.

For bag straps, cotton twill tape and Petersham ribbon have been used to add strength. Cords serve as drawstrings and handles; these are available in various colours and thicknesses.

TECHNIQUES

The majority of the projects in this book involve basic sewing techniques, both by hand and machine. In this section, you will find some basic instructions and tips to help you make your bags and purses as neat and professional-looking as possible.

PREPARING TO SEW

MARKING FABRIC

When a project is made up of squares, rectangles and strips of fabric, measurements are given within the pattern instructions and you will need to measure and mark out these pieces on your fabric. Use a ruler for straight lines, and mark out shapes using tailor's chalk or a dressmaker's chalk pencil, both of which produce a line that can be rubbed out afterwards. Use a colour that shows up on the fabric. In most cases, when the marks will be hidden in the seams or on the wrong side of the fabric, you can use an ordinary pencil instead. More complex shapes appear as templates at the back of the book; some can be traced, and others photocopied.

INTERFACING

To add substance to the cotton fabrics used in the book, in most cases a fusible fabric stiffener (interfacing) has been applied to the fabric pieces before they are assembled. The type and weight you need is specified in the project. Identify which side of the interfacing is adhesive and place this side face down on the wrong side of the fabric. Place a piece of baking parchment on top, to protect the base plate of the iron. You may also wish to place some scrap fabric in between the fabric and the ironing board, to protect your ironing-board cover. Press with an iron set on medium heat; try not to glide the iron, as this may cause the two layers of fabric and interfacing to shift. Hold the iron in the same position for about 10 seconds before lifting it, then move to another area, and repeat. The heat from the iron will bond the interfacing to the fabric.

BASTING (TACKING) AND GATHERING

Basting is used to join layers of fabric together, or to fix pieces of fabric in position prior to sewing. Use a long running stitch for basting. Start and finish with a couple of stitches worked over each other to secure the end of the thread, and work the stitches within the seam allowance. When the seam or hem has been permanently sewn by machine, remove the basting stitches. For gathering, use the same stitch, but the stitches should be shorter and closer together; it is advisable to use two strands of thread.

HAND SEWING

SLIPSTITCH

When sewing the lining of a bag, leave a gap of about 4in (10cm), or less if it is a small bag, in your line of stitching along one edge. Reverse stitch (backstitch) at either side of the gap to avoid tearing the seam when you turn the work right side out. Fold in the raw edges on either side of the gap, then close the gap by slipstitching. To do this, secure the thread, and pick up a small section of fabric along the fold on one side, using the tip of the needle. Then pick up a small amount of fabric on the other side. Repeat all along the opening, and fasten off.

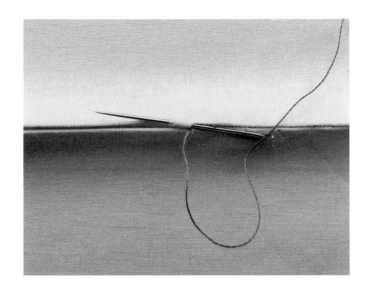

BLANKET STITCH

This stitch is usually used for edging but can be worked as a decorative embroidery stitch. It is also used for buttonholes, with the stitches worked very close together.

Push the needle up through the fabric on the top stitchline and bring it back out directly below on the bottom line. This creates a small loop at the top. Take the needle up through the loop and pull to tighten; the vertical thread is now held in place by a small horizontal bar. You can choose the height of the stitch as you insert the needle down into the fabric shape, and also the space between stitches.

SPLIT STITCH

This stitch is very useful for outlining or for describing straight or curved lines. Thread the needle with the desired number of strands of embroidery thread. Bring the needle up through the fabric at the beginning of the line, then down a little way along. Keep the stitches reasonably short: about $1/8$–$3/16$in (4-5mm) in length. Bring the needle up through the centre of the stitch you just made. Take the needle back through the fabric a little way along the line. Repeat the process for the whole length of the line.

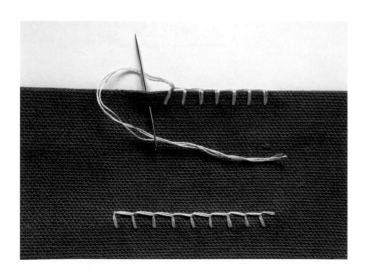

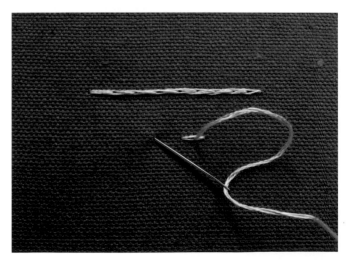

MACHINE SEWING

Most of the stitching for these bag and purse projects is done on a sewing machine with a straight stitch; a zigzag stitch is also useful for neatening raw edges. It is essential that your sewing-machine needle is the right size for the fabric – size 80 for medium-weight cotton – and that it is sharp.

SETTING UP

Set up the machine where there is plenty of light and you can sit comfortably. Make sure that the machine is threaded correctly and that the threads from the needle and bobbin are placed away from you, towards the back of the machine. Turn the hand wheel towards you, to lower the needle into the fabric; this will help to prevent the threads from tangling. Keep scraps of the fabric you are working with to test out your stitch size and tension before starting to sew your project. If you have a speed restriction facility on your machine, use this to improve control and accuracy when sewing curves or topstitching.

STRAIGHT STITCH

This stitch is used for flat seams and topstitching, and for hemming. You can alter the length of straight stitch – a long stitch can be used for gathering or basting. At the start and end of a line of stitching, backstitch for a few stitches; this will prevent the stitching from coming undone.

TOPSTITCHING

Topstitching creates a crisp finish and holds layers neatly and securely in place, especially on seams and at the top edges of bags.

Press the seam to one side. Topstitch parallel to the seamline; the distance from this line is variable but on a seam it is usually a smaller measurement than the seam allowance, so that the raw edges of the seam are trapped under the topstitching.

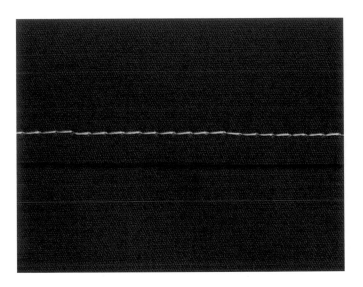

Topstitching is also used to attach pieces such as straps. Stitch close to the edge of the strap. It is advisable to stitch extra lines of topstitching in the form of a cross, to help to secure and reinforce the strap.

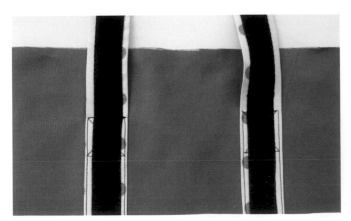

FRENCH SEAM

A French seam is an efficient way to prevent the raw edges of a seam from fraying. This technique produces a neat finish that is ideal for items that get a lot of wear or are reversible, for unlined items, or where the seam will be visible.

1 Place the two pieces of fabric to be joined wrong sides together. Pin or tack before stitching a straight seam along this edge, with a ¼in (6mm) seam allowance.

2 Turn the seam with the work wrong sides out. Push out the seam to make it as neat and sharp as possible. Press the seam.

3 Pin and baste, then stitch a ⅜in (1cm) seam. You will now have encased the raw edges completely within the seam. Give the seam a final press to one side.

ZIGZAG STITCH

This stitch is used along raw edges to help reduce fraying, especially on seams. Zigzag stitch can also be used decoratively, and for making machine buttonholes.

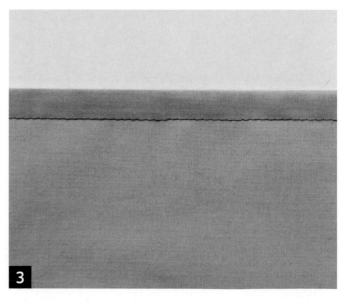

ADDITIONAL TECHNIQUES

BINDING EDGES

Two-step binding is the preferred method for an uneven edge, multiple layers of fabric, and for binding corners and curves.

1 Open out the binding and line up the raw edges of the binding and the fabric. Pin and baste, then stitch along the foldline.

2 Fold the bias binding over, to enclose the raw edges, and slipstitch the other long folded edge of the binding on the seamline.

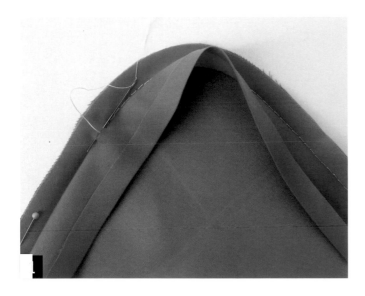

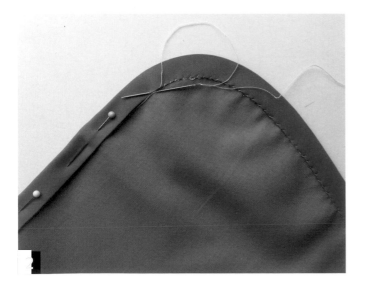

ONE-STEP BINDING

One-step binding works best on a straight edge of firm fabric. Fold the binding in half down its length and press. Place the folded binding over the edge of the fabric, to enclose it completely. Pin and stitch close to the lower edge of the binding, checking on the wrong side that the stitching has captured both long edges.

CLIPPING CORNERS AND CURVES

Corners should be cut across at an angle so they are sharp when the work is turned right side out.

On curved seams, cut 'V' shapes into the seam close to the stitchline to make the seam smooth when the work is turned right side out. Snip very carefully with small, sharp scissors to avoid cutting through the stitches by mistake.

QUILTING

Quilting helps to hold layers of fabric together, especially when they have wadding or fleece sandwiched in between. Draw the lines to be quilted using an erasable marker or chalk. When quilting by hand, use a running stitch, and use a long straight stitch when quilting by machine.

HOW TO PUT IN A ZIP

This shows the basic technique of placing a zip between two pieces of fabric.

1 With fabric right side up, place the zip face down, aligning one edge of the tape with one edge of the fabric. Baste.

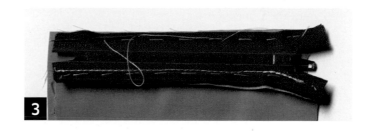

2 Using a zipper foot on your sewing machine, stitch the tape in place.

3 Position the other zip tape edge along the edge of the other piece of fabric, right sides together. Baste and stitch, as before.

4 Open out the work and press the folds of fabric, taking care not to let the hotplate of the iron touch the plastic teeth on the zip.

5 Topstitch along both sides, approximately ⅛in (3mm) from the folded edges.

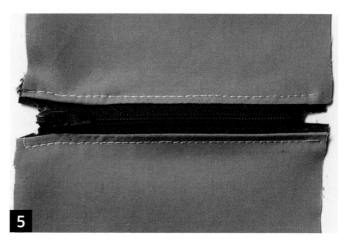

FINISHING TOUCHES

COVERED BUTTONS

Covered buttons are easy to make and look very professional, whether you use a matching or a contrasting fabric. You can buy plastic or metal self-covering buttons in a range of sizes. This technique can also be used for covering press studs; in order for the two parts to connect, you will need to pierce a hole in the centre of each fabric circle, using a sharp point.

1 Cut a circle of fabric; the diameter will be guided by the size of the button, and templates are usually supplied when you buy a pack of self-covering buttons. Sew a running stitch around the edge of the fabric. Place the button top face down on the wrong side.

2 Pull up the end of the thread to gather the fabric. Fasten off securely.

3 Push the button back securely in place, covering the edges of the fabric.

HOW TO STITCH A BUTTONHOLE

1 Mark a line on the fabric, the same length as the diameter of the button. Cut along the line, using sharp scissors.

2 Sew an outline of running stitch around the slit.

3 Now work blanket stitches all around the slit, making sure the stitches are close together and with no gaps in between.

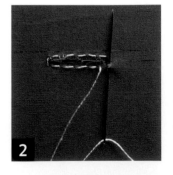

ELASTIC BUTTON LOOP

A loop of elastic makes a good fastening in conjunction with a button or toggle. Sew it into the seam for neatness.

1 Cut a length of elastic that will fit snugly around the button and add ⅜–¾in (1–2cm) extra, to fit the ends into the seam. Bring the two ends together, to make a loop. With the loop facing inwards, pin the cut ends in position on the right side of the fabric.

2 Place the corresponding piece of fabric on top, so that the right sides are together, and stitch the seam, trapping the ends of the elastic inside.

3 Turn the fabric right sides out and press along the seam; avoid letting the hot iron come into contact with the elastic.

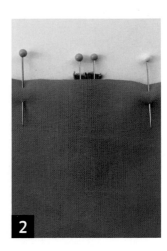

ROULEAUX

A rouleau (plural: rouleaux) is a narrow tube of fabric. A short length can be used for a button loop and fixed in place in the same way as the elastic loop above. A longer length – commonly used for shoestring straps on dresses and lingerie – makes an elegant strap for an evening bag. Making one can be fiddly, but the task is simplified if you use a loop turner: a long metal pin with a ring on one end and a clip on the other. Cut a strip of fabric to the length required and twice the width of the finished strap, then add ¾in (2cm) for the seam. Fold in half lengthways, right sides together, aligning the long edges, and stitch a ⅜in (1cm) seam. Trim the seam allowance to 3⁄16in (5mm). Insert the loop turner into the tube of fabric and attach the clip to the end of the seam, then pull the loop turner back through the tube.

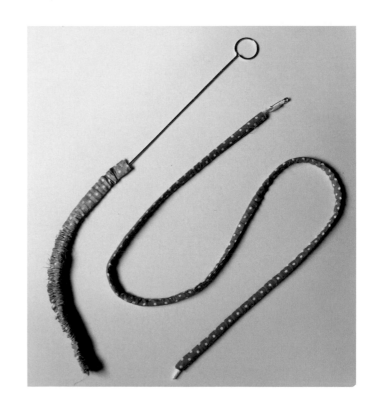

ON THE MOVE

TOTE BAG

This all-purpose unlined bag has a rectangular base, making it deceptively capacious, yet it is lightweight and folds flat to fit in a pocket, purse or glove compartment. Fill it with groceries or use it for home storage – this tote has a multitude of uses.

You will need
2 fat quarters of fabric
About 16 x 5in (40 x 13cm) of heavyweight
    fusible interfacing
Tailor's chalk or chalk pencil
Ruler
Pins
Dressmaking scissors
Iron and ironing board
Sewing machine
Thread to match fabric

NOTE: The bag is sized to make the most of two fat quarters, with the minimum of wastage. You could use a different patterned fabric for the back and front.

Finished size is roughly:
15¼ x 10½ x 4¾in (39 x 26 x 12cm)

1 Cut two pieces of fabric measuring 20 x 16in (50 x 40cm). These pieces will form the front, back and base of the bag.

2 From the remaining fabric, cut two rectangles 16 x 3in (40 x 8cm) for the handles.

3 Cut four strips of fusible interfacing, each measuring 15½ x 1¼in (39 x 3cm). Place one of the strips of interfacing ⅜in (1cm) below the top (short) edge of the bag front, on the wrong side, and fix in place using a hot iron. Do the same with the bag back.

4 Fuse the two remaining strips of interfacing to the wrong side of the bag handles, down the centre of the fabric.

5 Place the bag back and front right sides together and stitch the side seams and base of the bag with a ⅜in (1cm) seam allowance. Press the side seams open.

6 To make the rectangular base, on one of the lower corners, align the side seam and base seam and press flat. From the corner, measure 2¼in (6cm) along the seam and draw a line across at right angles to the seam. Stitch along this line, then trim off the corner ⅜in (1cm) from the seam. Repeat with the other corner.

7 On the top edge of the bag, fold ⅜in (1cm) to the wrong side and press, then fold over 1¼in (3cm) and press again, to form a double hem.

8 On the handles, fold one long edge by ¼in (6mm) to the wrong side and press, then fold both long edges of fabric over the interfacing, to the centre, with the folded edge overlapping the raw edge. Pin, then stitch down the centre, close to the folded edge.

9 Mark the centre top of the bag, on the back and the front, then place ends of handles halfway between the marked point and side seam. Make sure the centre seam of the handle is on the underside when you do this. Tuck ⅜in (1cm) of each end of each handle under the hem and pin in place.

10 Stitch the hem ⅛in (3mm) from the folded edge on the inside, then fold the handles upwards and press. Topstitch ⅛in (3mm) from the top edge of the bag (see page 16).

Tip

When applying fusible materials to fabric, use a hot iron without steam, and lay a piece of baking parchment between the material and the iron, to prevent any adhesive sticking to the iron. You may wish to place a piece of baking parchment on the ironing board as well, to protect the ironing-board cover.

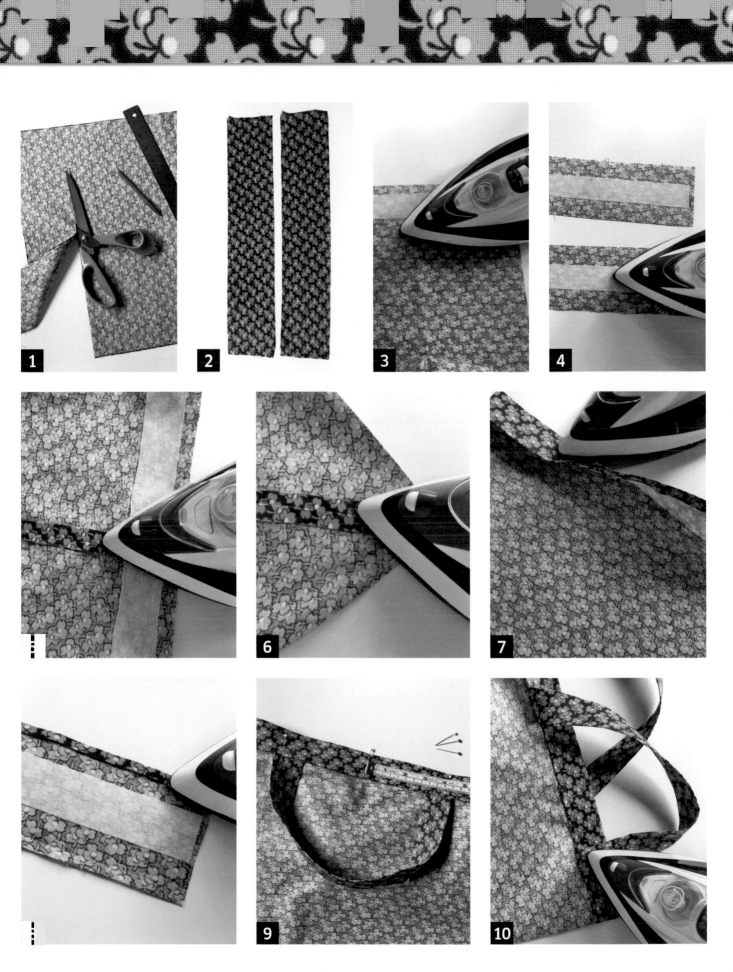

BEACH BAG

Perfect for carrying all the paraphernalia for a day at the beach or pool, this roomy bag has a firm base and straps for holding a rolled towel or beach mat. It has a couple of clasps for attaching small items so they don't get lost in the sand.

You will need
1 fat quarter of main fabric
1 fat quarter of contrast fabric
2 fat quarters of plain cotton fabric, for lining and base
About ½yd (45cm) of fusible fleece
15⅜ x 5¼in (39 x 13cm) of fusible foam
Tailor's chalk or chalk pencil
Ruler
Dressmaking scissors
Pins
Iron and ironing board
Sewing machine
Thread to match fabric
48in (1.2m) of 1in (25mm)-wide cotton herringbone twill tape
Sewing needle
Thread for basting
7in (18cm) of ¾in (2cm)-wide hook-and-loop fastening
2 lobster-trigger swivel clasps

Finished size is roughly:
10½ x 15 x 4¾in (27 x 38 x 12cm)

1 From the main fabric, measure and cut two rectangles 21¼in x 8¾in (54 x 22cm). From the contrast fabric, cut two rectangles measuring 21¼ x 4in (54 x 10cm) and four strips 21¼ x 2¼in (54 x 6cm). From the plain fabric, cut two rectangles measuring 21¼ x 12in (54 x 30cm) and two pieces 15¾ x 5½in (40 x 14cm) for the base. From fusible fleece, cut two pieces measuring 21 x 11½in (53 x 29cm), one 15⅜ x 5¼in (39 x 13cm) and two 21 x 2in (53 x 5cm).

2 To make the handles, fuse the narrow strip of fleece to two of the strips of contrast fabric with a hot iron. Pair each one with the two remaining strips and stitch down both long edges with a ⅜in (1cm) seam. Turn right sides out.

3 Place the ends of the handles on one piece of main fabric and place one of the larger strips of contrast on top, aligning the long edges. Join with a ⅜in (1cm) seam. Do the same with the other piece of main fabric and the other handle.

4 Open out and press the seam towards the main fabric. On the right side, topstitch across the width of the bag (see page 16), ³⁄₁₆in (5mm) from the seamline. Topstitch the base of each handle, close to the seamline, to ensure it is attached firmly in place. On the wrong side, fuse the fleece in place with a hot iron.

5 Cut four 10in (25cm) lengths of cotton tape for the straps. Pin the ends of two of these lengths of tape on the front, placing the edges 5½in (14cm) in from the sides.

6 Fuse the piece of fusible foam to one of the base pieces with a hot iron. Pin this base centrally to the long edge of the front, covering the ends of the tape. Stitch the base with a ⅜in (1cm) seam, beginning and ending the seam ⅜in (1cm) from the side edges of the base.

7 Stitch the other long edge of the base to the other main piece of fabric, once again sandwiching the two ends of the tape in the seam. Stitch the corner seams. Clip the corners (see page 18) and turn right sides out.

8 Apply the last piece of fusible fleece to the remaining base piece. Then join all lining pieces. Join the two long edges of the base to the bottom edges of the front and back. Join the side seams, then stitch the two corner seams.

9 On the top edge of both the bag and lining, fold ½in (1.25cm) to the wrong side, press and baste. Cut the remaining cotton tape into two equal lengths, pass one end through the ring on a lobster clasp, then baste the tape ends to the inside of the outer bag, on the seamline. Do the same with the other clasp, on the opposite side seam. Slipstitch (see page 15) the folded edge of the lining to the folded edge of the bag, then stitch two lines of topstitching all round.

10 Stitch a 3½in (9cm) strip of the hook-and-loop tape to the ends of the four tapes on the base, folding under the end of each piece of tape, to neaten.

1

2

3

4

5

6

8

9

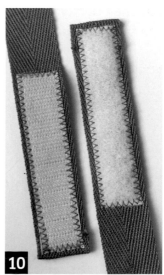

10

SIGHTSEEING BACKPACK

This practical bag has a drawstring and a flap to keep your belongings secure, two straps so that it sits comfortably on your back, and a loop for hanging it up. It also has two exterior side pockets to keep drinks and other items handy when on the move.

Find the template on page 133

You will need
2 fat quarters of main fabric
2 fat quarters of contrast fabric
2 fat quarters of plain cotton fabric, for lining
32 x 20in (80 x 50cm) of heavyweight fusible interfacing
32 x 20in (80 x 50cm) of fusible fleece
About 2yd (1.7m) of 1in (25mm)-wide cotton braid
10in (25cm) of elastic
About 1½yd (1.4m) of cord, ¼in (6mm) diameter
Sew-on magnetic closure, or large press stud, 1in (2.5cm) diameter
Pencil
Paper-cutting scissors
Pins
Dressmaking scissors
Sewing machine
Sewing needle
Thread to match fabric and braid
Thread for basting
Iron and ironing board

Finished size is roughly:
13¼ x 10½ x 3½in (34 x 27 x 9cm)

1 Cut the following from the main and lining fabrics: two rectangles 13¾ x 11½in (35 x 29cm), two 13¾ x 3½in (35 x 9cm) and one 11½ x 4⅜in (29 x 11cm). From main fabric, cut four strips 15¾ x 3⅛in (40 x 8cm). From contrast, cut two 10in (25cm) squares for the pockets, and two 15¾ x 3¼in (40 x 8.5cm) pieces for the casing.

2 Cut two rectangles 13½ x 11in (34 x 28cm), two 13½ x 3⅛in (34 x 8cm), one 4 x 1½in (10 x 4cm) from the fusible fleece and interfacing. Use the template on page 133 to cut one flap from contrast fabric, lining, fusible fleece and interfacing. Trim away 3⁄16in (5mm) all around the fleece and interfacing. Fuse the interfacing to the wrong side of the lining pieces and the fleece to the wrong side of the main fabric pieces.

3 From the interfacing, cut two strips each 30½ x 1½in (77 x 4cm) for the straps and one strip 30½ x 3in (77 x 7.5cm) for the casing. Join two pairs of fabric strips with a ⅜in (1cm) seam to make two straps. Fuse the interfacing to the wrong side of each, placing it centrally. Fold in the fabric edges to meet in the centre, and press. Join the two pieces of the casing with a ⅜in (1cm) seam and fuse the interfacing to the wrong side. Press a ⅜in (1cm) double hem at each end.

4 Cut two 30¾in (78cm) lengths of braid and pin down the centre of each strap. Stitch in place, close to the edges of the braid. Pin and baste one end of each strap to the main fabric back piece, 1in (2.5cm) in from the side edges.

5 Place the two flap pieces right sides together and stitch, leaving a turning gap. Clip corners (see page 18), then turn right side out. Pin the ends of the remaining length of braid to the centre of the top edge, to form a hanging loop. Place the flap centrally on top, with the free ends of the two straps on either side; pin and baste.

6 On one edge on each pocket, fold ¼in (6mm) to the wrong side, and press, then fold a further ½in (1.25cm) and press again. Stitch close to the bottom fold, to create a casing. Insert a 5in (12.75cm) length of elastic in each casing and stitch the ends in place on either side. On the opposite edge, stitch a gathering thread. Line up the gathered edge of each pocket to the base of each side. Pull up the gathering threads until the bottom of the pocket fits. Baste.

7 Stitch the side seams, finishing ⅜in (1cm) short of the bottom edge on each seam. Do the same with the lining. Press seams open.

8 Pin, baste and stitch the bag base to the bag. Do the same with the lining.

9 Slip the lining inside the bag, with wrong sides together. Baste the top edges together. With a zigzag stitch, machine stitch all around the top edge, to hold the layers together.

10 Line up the centre seam of the casing with the centre of the flap and place the two hemmed ends together at the centre of the front of the bag. Pin and baste in place, and stitch with a ⅝in (1.5cm) seam allowance. Press the seam to one side, towards the casing.

11 Fold under ⅜in (1cm) on the other long edge of the casing, fold to the inside and slipstitch the fold to the seamline inside the bag (see page 15). Topstitch ¼in (6mm) from the bottom edge of the casing all round (see page 16). Topstitch again, ¼in (6mm) from the first line of stitching. Thread the cord through the casing, with the ends emerging at the front opening.

12 Stitch one half of the magnetic closure securely to the inside of the flap, close to the edge, and the other on the front of the bag.

DOG WALKER'S BAG

Suspend this handy holdall from one handle on a peg or coat rack to store leads, treats and plastic bags for your canine companion. It transforms quickly and easily into a carry-all for dog walking when it's time for you both to go out.

You will need
1 fat quarter of fabric
1 fat quarter of plain cotton fabric, for lining
22 x 11in (55 x 27cm) of fusible fleece
1½yd (1.4m) of ⅝in (16mm)-wide Petersham ribbon
1½yd (1.4m) of 1in (25mm)-wide cotton herringbone twill tape
2¾in (7cm) of ¾in (20mm)-wide hook-and-loop fastening
20 x 12in (50 x 30cm) of 12-gauge clear vinyl fabric
3½yd (3.2m) of 1in (25mm)-wide bias binding
3 zips, 10in (25cm) long
Tailor's chalk or chalk pencil
Set square
Ruler
Pins
Dressmaking scissors
Iron and ironing board
Permanent marker, such as ballpoint pen
Sewing machine
Sewing needle
Thread to match fabric

NOTE: Vinyl can be tricky to work with. If creased, it can be ironed using a pressing cloth; when you do this it becomes very floppy but it firms up again when it cools. Pinning can make holes in the vinyl, so place any pins within the seam allowance, to minimize damage, or use clips instead.

Finished size is roughly:
21 x 10½in (53 x 27cm)

1 Measure and cut from main fabric, lining and fusible fleece rectangles 21¼ x 10½in (54 x 26.5cm). Use the set square to ensure accurate right angles. Trim off a ⅜in (1cm) strip from one long edge and one short edge of the fleece and place it centrally on the wrong side of the main fabric. Fuse in place, using a hot iron.

2 Pin Petersham ribbon down the centre of the cotton tape and stitch down both sides. Cut two 15in (38cm) lengths, for the handles. Turn under ½in (15mm) at each end, and press.

3 Pin the handles in place on the right side of the main fabric. At the top end, position the folded end of one handle 5in (12.75cm) down from the top and 2¾in (7cm) in from each side.

4 Position the second handle 9½in (24cm) from the bottom edge and 2¾in (7cm) in from the sides. Stitch in place, stitching a diagonal cross to reinforce the handle. Trim the remaining tape to 19in (48cm). Fold under ½in (1.25cm) on each end. Cut a ¾in (2cm) square of the hook part of the hook-and-loop fastening and stitch it in place on the right side at one end. Pin this end between the ends of the handle at the top end of the bag. Run the tape down the centre and pin it between the ends of the other handle. Stitch down both sides and across, where indicated by the pins, leaving the end free. Stitch a 2¾in (7cm) strip of the loop part of the fastening to the underside of this end.

5 Cut four rectangles of vinyl: one 10½ x 6¾in (26.5 x 17.5cm); two 10½ x 5⅛in (26.5 x 13cm); and one 10½ x 2¾in (26.5 x 7cm). Using the one-step binding method (see page 18), bind both edges of the two medium pieces of vinyl, and one long edge on each of the narrow and wide pieces.

6 Stitch zips between the bound edges (see How to put in a zip, page 19), thereby joining all the vinyl pieces into one long piece that will form pockets. Trim off the ends of the zips level with the edges of vinyl.

7 Place the zippered piece of vinyl on top of the lining, both with right sides up. Pin the two together, placing the pins in the zip tape to avoid making holes in the vinyl. The narrowest strip of vinyl is not a pocket; position this at the top. Stitch along the top edge of the binding on each zip, between the existing stitchlines, then baste all layers together, by hand or machine, ³⁄₁₆in (5mm) from edges.

8 Place the lining fabric on the outer section, wrong sides together, and pin, once again positioning pins in the zip tapes. Place a round object such as a small dish on each corner and draw around it. Cut along the drawn lines, to create rounded corners.

9 Bind all round, using the two-step method (see page 18). Open out the binding and line up the raw edge with the edge of the fabric. Stitch by machine, or by hand using backstitch.

10 Fold the binding over the edge and stitch the other folded edge in place. Topstitch all round (see page 16) and fold in the ends to create a neat join.

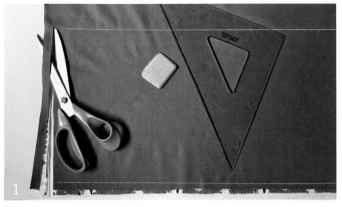
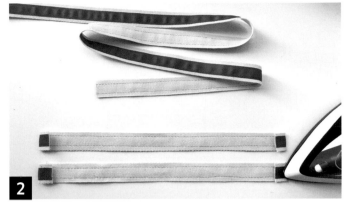

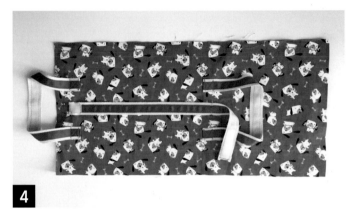

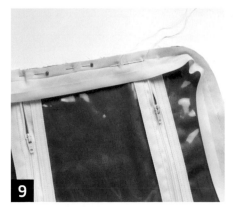
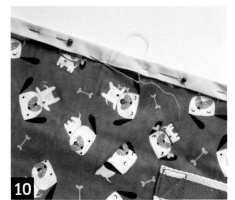

BOTTLE CARRIER

Keep this handy bottle bag in the car to take on shopping trips, or use it for picnics. It holds four bottles: the dividers keep them upright and prevent them from knocking against each other. The bag folds flat when empty, making it even easier to store.

You will need
1 fat quarter of main fabric
2 fat quarters of contrast fabric, for lining
51in (1.3m) of medium-weight fusible interfacing
48in (1.2m) of 1in (25mm)-wide cotton herringbone twill tape
67in (1.7m) of ¾in (20mm)-wide bias binding
Tailor's chalk or chalk pencil
Ruler
Pins
Dressmaking scissors
Sewing machine
Sewing needle
Thread to match fabric
Iron and ironing board

Finished size is roughly:
12 x 7 x 7in (30.5 x 18 x 18cm)

1 From the main fabric and one of the fat quarters of lining, cut two rectangles 15¾ x 7in (40 x 18cm) and two rectangles 12¼ x 7in (31 x 18cm). From the other fat quarter of lining, cut four 9½in (24cm) squares.

2 From fusible interfacing, cut four rectangles 15⅜ x 6⅝in (39 x 17cm), four 12 x 6⅝in (30 x 17cm) and four 9in (23cm) squares. Fuse one piece of interfacing on to each of the corresponding pieces of fabric, both main fabric and lining.

3 Join the two large rectangles that form the back and front of the bag by lining up two short ends, right sides together, and stitching with a ⅝in (1.5cm) seam allowance. Press the seam open. Do the same with the lining pieces.

4 Place the two joined pieces of main fabric and lining wrong sides together, with all edges and the seams aligned, then pin and baste the layers together, by hand or machine, all round, within the ⅜in (1cm) seam allowance. Do the same with the four side pieces, pairing one piece of main fabric with one piece of lining.

5 Take two of the squares of lining fabric and place right sides together. Pin, baste and stitch along two opposite sides with a ⅜in (1cm) seam allowance. Do the same with the other two squares of lining fabric. Turn right sides out and press. Topstitch the seamed sides, ¼in (6mm) from the edge (see page 16).

6 To create the dividers, place the two pieces with raw edges matching; these will be sandwiched into the side seams at a later stage. Pin the layers together, then measure and mark a line down the centre. Stitch along this line from top to bottom.

7 Place the raw edge of one of the dividers along one of the long side edges of the bag, with the base of the divider 1¼in (3cm) above the lower edge of the side piece. Pin or clip in place, then baste within the seam allowance. Place the other edge of the next divider along the opposite edge. Pin or clip the remaining two edges of the dividers to the other side piece, and baste.

8 Pin or clip the sides to the front and back piece, matching the ends of the centre seam to the centre of each side piece. Baste, then stitch together.

9 Cut the binding in half. Open up one piece and line up the long edge with the raw edge of the seam. Pin the binding in place, then stitch along the foldline.

10 Fold the binding over, to enclose the seam, and slipstitch (see page 15) the folded edge to cover the seamline. Ease the binding around corners, making a small pleat if necessary.

11 From the remaining main or lining fabric, cut two strips 13¾ x 2¼in (35 x 6cm). Sew the short ends together to make a ring and press the seams open. On both long edges, fold ⅜in (1cm) to the wrong side and press. Use this strip to bind the top edge of the bag.

12 Cut the tape into two equal lengths and baste each one to the bag, one on the back and one on the front, to make handles. To do this, fold under 1in (2.5cm) on each end and position approximately 2in (5cm) down from the top of the bag, with the edge of the tape 1in (2.5cm) in from the corner; do the same with the other end of the handle. Sew in place, stitching a diagonal cross to make them really secure.

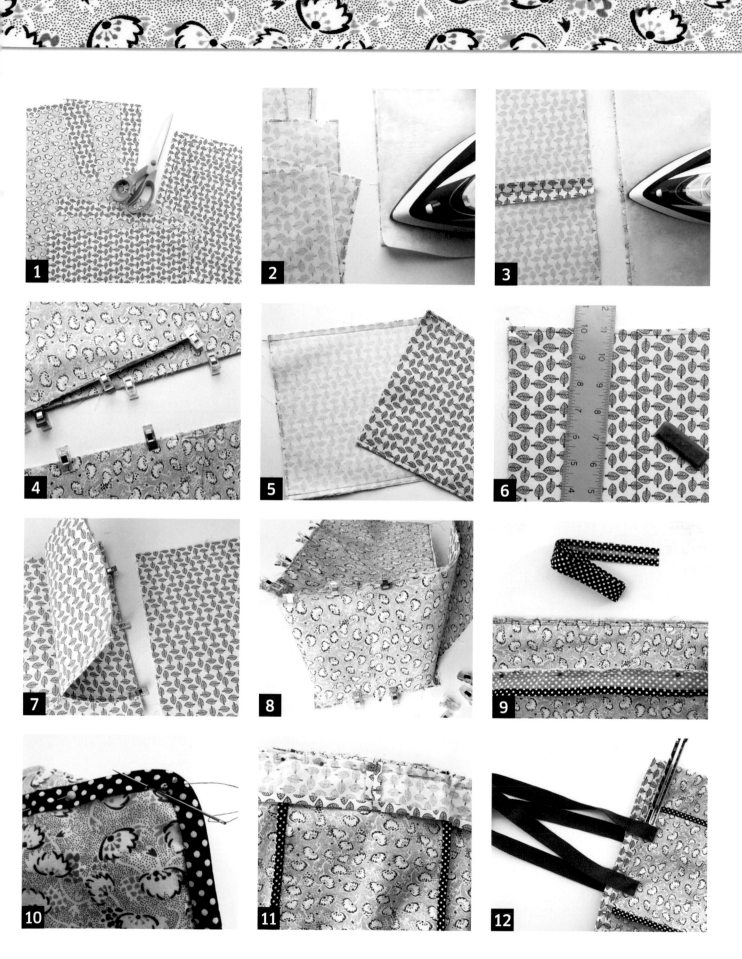

BAGS FOR ESSENTIALS

COIN PURSE

Use this handy coin purse to hold your loose change. It's also great for stowing headphones and USB cables, chargers or any other small odds and ends in one secure and easy-to-access place when you're on the move.

You will need
1 fat quarter of main fabric
1 fat quarter of contrast fabric, for lining
13 x 11in (33 x 28cm) of fusible fleece
About 5in (12.5cm) of ⅜in (1cm)-wide ribbon (optional)
Tape measure or ruler
Dressmaking scissors
Iron and ironing board
Pins
Sewing needle
Knitting needle or similar for poking out corners
Thread for basting
Sewing machine
Thread to match fabric and bias binding

NOTE: The seam allowance is ¼in (6mm), unless otherwise stated.

Finished size is roughly:
5¼ x 5½in (13 x 14cm)

1 Measure and cut two 6¾ x 6in (17 x 15cm) pieces of main fabric and two of contrast. Cut four pieces of fusible fleece, each measuring 6¼ x 5½in (16 x 14cm).

2 Use a hot iron to fuse one piece of fusible fleece to each of the fabric pieces.

3 Place the zip right side up on the right side of one of the lining pieces, with the edge of the tape aligned with one long edge of the lining. Pin and baste. Place a main fabric piece wrong side up on top, aligning the top edges. Pin and baste through all layers. With the zipper foot on your sewing machine, stitch about ¼in (6mm) from the edge. Open out and press.

4 Place the second lining piece right side up and place the other zip tape along the top edge. Pin and baste. Then place the second main piece on top, wrong side up, baste and stitch, as before.

5 Open out and press. Topstitch the edges alongside the zip for a neat finish, with the seamline ³/₁₆in (5mm) from the folded edge (see page 16).

6 Open the zip, then open out the purse, matching the two main pieces together, and the two lining pieces together. Align the seams, having the zip teeth facing towards the lining.

7 Pin the edges of fabric together, baste, then stitch, leaving a turning gap of about 3in (7.5cm) on the bottom edge of the lining. Clip the corners (see page 18), turn right sides out, and push out the corners using a knitting needle.

8 Fold the raw edges inside the opening in the lining and slipstitch the folded edges together (see page 15). Push the lining inside the purse.

Tip
To make a zip pull (optional), push both ends of a piece of ribbon into the hole in the metal zip and knot the ends together.

PASSPORT WALLET

Keep your passport and related documents in this handy wallet and you are ready to go at a moment's notice. This project requires a relatively small amount of fabric: if you use the same fabric for the exterior and the lining, you can make three wallets from one fat quarter.

Find the template on page 132

You will need
1 fat quarter of main fabric
1 fat quarter of contrast fabric, for lining
8¾ x 7in (22 x 18cm) of buckram
8¾ x 7in (22 x 18cm) of 12-gauge clear vinyl
48in (1.2m) of ½in (12mm)-wide bias binding
Tape measure or ruler
Paper-cutting scissors
Pencil
Pins
Dressmaking scissors
Sewing machine
Sewing needle
Thread to match fabric
Snap fastener
Iron and ironing board

Finished size is roughly:
8¾ x 7in (22 x 18cm) when open;
4½ x 7in (11.5 x 18cm) when closed

1 Draw a line across the centre of the buckram. Place the main fabric and contrast fabric on top of each other, pin the buckram on top and cut out both fabrics about ½in (1.25cm) bigger than the buckram all round.

2 Place the buckram on the wrong side of the lining fabric piece, pin in place and pin and stitch the two together up the centre line. Then stitch all around, very close to the edges of the buckram. Trim off excess fabric.

3 Place the lining on top of the piece of main fabric, pin, and stitch together, close to the edges. Trim off excess fabric.

4 Use the template on page 132 to make a paper pattern, and cut two pieces from the vinyl.

5 Bind each of the curved edges of the vinyl with bias binding (see page 18). Pin the vinyl pockets face up on the lining, matching the straight edges, and stitch all around.

6 Bind around the edge of the wallet with bias binding, making a neat mitre on each corner.

7 Cut a 4¾in (12cm) length of bias binding, fold it in half, right sides together, and stitch down both sides. Trim the seam allowance and turn right sides out. Fold in the raw edges on the unstitched end and slipstitch closed (see page 15). Stitch this end to the edge of the binding on the centre back edge of the wallet.

8 Use leftover bias binding to cover both parts of the snap fastener, following the instructions for doing this on page 20. Stitch the top part of the snap fastener to the folded end of the tab, and the lower part to the centre front edge of the wallet, about ³⁄₁₆in (5mm) from the edge.

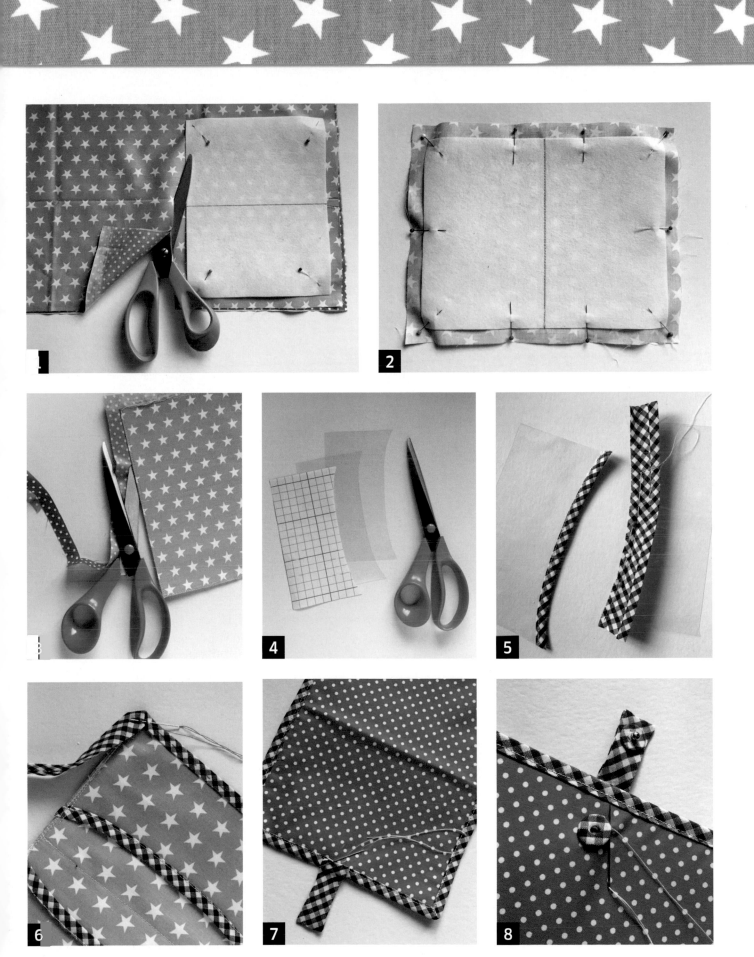

QUILTED GLASSES CASE

This handy slipcase will fit easily into the pocket of a shirt or jacket to keep sunglasses or reading glasses to hand. The quilting prevents the glasses from becoming scratched, and the case has a simple button fastening so they won't fall out.

Find the template on page 132

You will need
1 fat quarter of main fabric, with a regular print
1 fat quarter of contrast fabric, for lining
8in (20cm) square of medium-weight fusible interfacing
8in (20cm) square of fusible fleece
Tape measure or ruler
Pencil
Paper-cutting scissors
Pins
Dressmaking scissors
Iron and ironing board
Crewel needle
6-stranded embroidery thread, in three colours
3in (7.5cm) of ¼in (6mm)-wide elastic
Sewing needle
Thread for basting
Sewing machine
Thread to match fabric
⅝in (1.5cm) button

NOTE: The seam allowance is ⅜in (1cm), unless otherwise stated.

Finished size is roughly:
6 x 3in (15 x 7.5cm)

1 Using the template on page 132, cut two pieces each from the main fabric, contrast fabric, interfacing and fleece.

2 Apply the two pieces of interfacing to the wrong side of the contrast fabric; this will form the lining. Trim 1/16in (2mm) all round the pieces of fleece, and apply to the wrong side of the main fabric pieces.

3 Thread the crewel needle with two strands of embroidery thread and sew lines of running stitch, evenly spaced, all over the main fabric pieces, following the lines of the printed design. Make sure the needle goes through both the fabric and the fleece.

4 Fold the elastic in half and line up the ends with the centre top edge of one of the main pieces. Baste in place. Then pair the main pieces and lining pieces, and stitch across the short straight edge of each with a 3/8in (1cm) seam.

5 Open up each piece and press the seam to one side. Place the two pieces, wrong sides together, and stitch down the two long sides and the curved edge of the main pieces, leaving the opposite curved end open.

6 Cut across the corners and snip into the seam allowance on the curved edge (see page 18).

7 Turn right sides out and press under 1/4in (6mm) on the open curved edge of the lining. Slipstitch the folded edges together (see page 15).

8 Tuck the lining inside, on the top edge of the case, and press the fold with a small margin of lining fabric showing on the outside. With two strands of embroidery thread, sew a running stitch through all layers of fabric (or topstitch by machine if you prefer – see page 16).

9 Sew a button to the top front of the case, to correspond with the elastic loop.

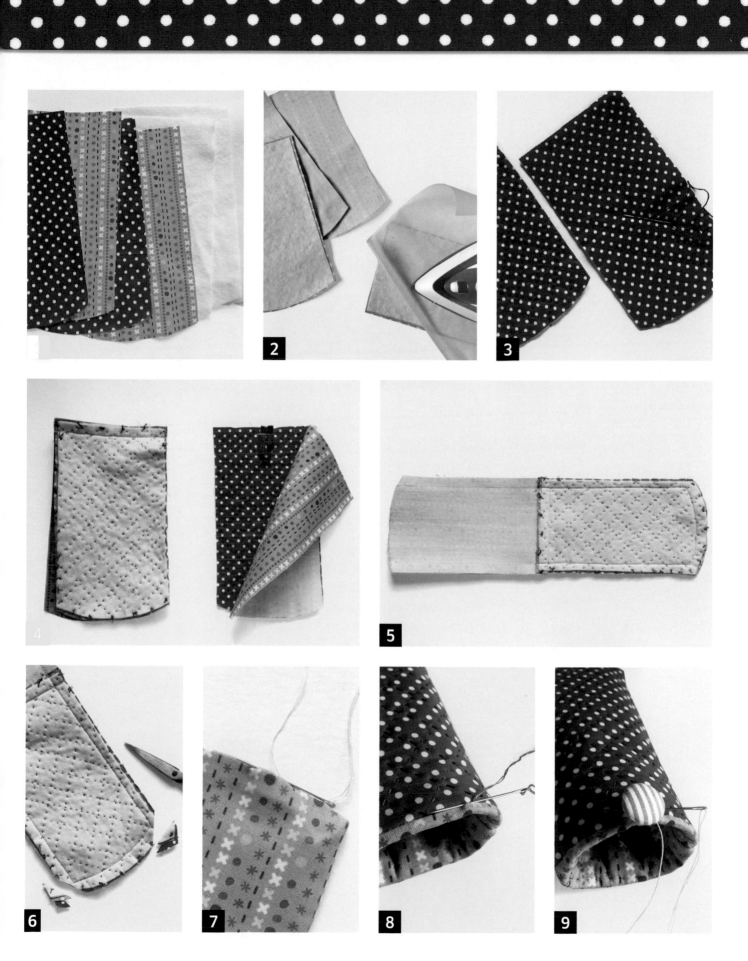

LAPTOP BAG

With an easy-access flap and lots of protective padding, this messenger-style bag is the perfect way to keep your precious laptop close to hand wherever you go. The bag fits a laptop measuring approximately 13 x 9½in (33 x 24cm).

You will need
2 fat quarters of main fabric
2 fat quarters of plain cotton fabric, for lining
24 x 16in (60 x 40cm) of fusible foam
14 x 10in (35 x 25cm) of fusible fleece
43 x 4in (110 x 10cm) of medium or heavyweight fusible interfacing
31½in (80cm) of ½in (12mm)-wide bias binding
Tape measure or ruler
Pins
Dressmaking scissors
Sewing needle
Thread for basting
Thread to match fabric and bias binding
Iron and ironing board
Baking parchment
Sewing machine

NOTE: The seam allowance is ⅝in (1.5cm) unless otherwise stated.

Finished size is roughly:
10 x 13½x 1¼in (25 x 34 x 3cm)

1 Measure and cut two rectangles 15³/₈ x 11in (39 x 28cm) from the main fabric, the lining and the fusible foam, to make the main bag. From the main fabric, lining and fleece, cut one rectangle measuring 12³/₄ x 9in (32.5 x 23cm) to make the flap. From the main fabric, cut two 21¹/₄ x 4¹/₈in (54 x 10.5cm) strips. From the fusible interfacing, cut a strip measuring 41¹/₄ x 3in (105 x 7.5cm).

2 Fuse the fleece to the wrong side of the main fabric flap piece.

3 Place the lining piece for the flap face up on top of the fused pieces. Pin the three layers together, then place a round object such as a small dish on the two lower corners. Draw around the edge, and cut along the line you have drawn to create a rounded corner.

4 Baste all layers together, removing the pins as you go, then bind the sides and bottom edge of the flap, using the two-step binding method (see page 18).

5 Place the fusible foam on the wrong side of the two main bag pieces and fuse it in place using a hot iron. Use baking parchment to protect the iron and ironing board.

Tip

The fabric strap is interfaced, then folded, creating a double layer of interfacing and therefore a very strong strap. For a softer finish you could use fusible fleece instead of interfacing.

6 Place the flap centrally on one of the main bag pieces, with right sides together and top edges aligned. Pin, baste and stitch together.

7 Stitch the two main bag pieces together at the sides and base, then create a corner gusset. To do this, align base and side seams on each corner, measure ⁵/₈in (1.5cm) from the corner and stitch across at this point.

8 Make up the lining in the same way: stitch base and side seams, and create a corner gusset on each side. Turn under ⁵/₈in (1.5cm) on the top edge of both bag outer and liner. Baste. Turn the bag right sides out and slip the lining inside, matching the side seams.

9 To make the strap, join the two pieces on one of the short edges, to create one long strip of fabric. Using a hot iron, fuse the strip of interfacing to the wrong side of the fabric. Fold ⁵/₈in (1.5cm) to the wrong side on each long edge. Fold the strap in half lengthways, with folded edges aligned, and press. Topstitch about ³/₁₆in (5mm) from the edge (see page 16).

10 Pin the ends of the strap to the side seams, sandwiched between the outer layer and the lining. Baste the layers together.

11 Slipstitch (see page 15) the top edge of the lining in place all around the top of the laptop bag. Then slipstitch along the seamline at the base of the flap.

12 Topstitch all around the top of the bag. Stitch a square shape at the base of the strap on each side, as reinforcement.

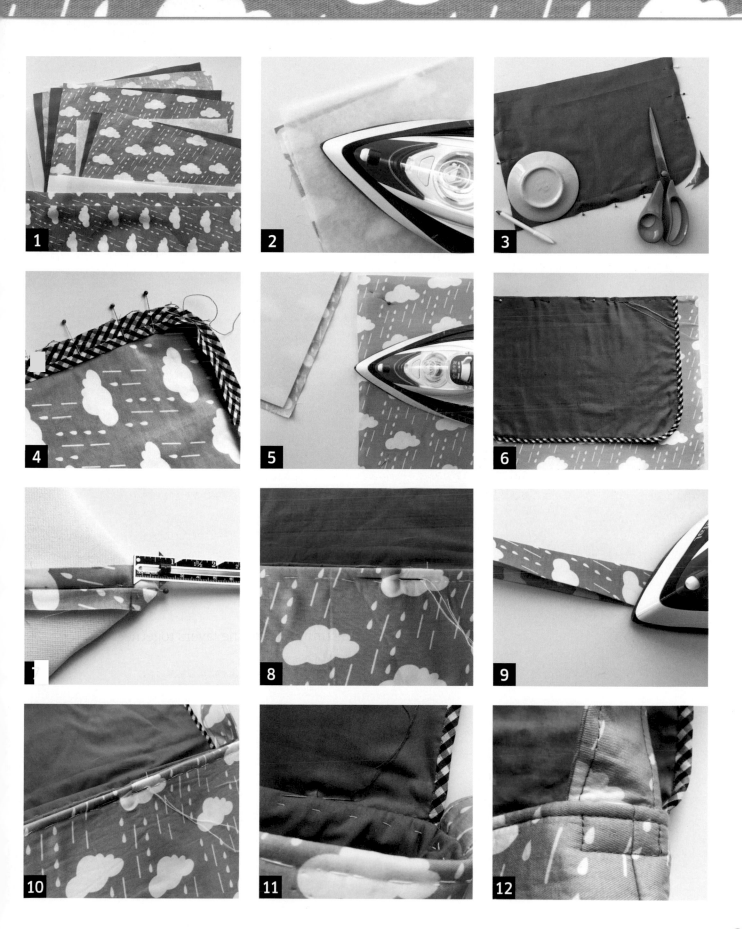

SHOULDER BAG

This shoulder bag is roomy enough for all the essentials of daily life. Choose contrasting patterned fabrics and a plain bright colour for the lining. There's a little pocket on the outside but otherwise this bag is nice and simple – to make and to use.

Find the templates on pages
134–5

You will need
1 fat quarter of main fabric
1 fat quarter of contrast fabric
1 fat quarter of plain cotton fabric, for lining
32 x 16in (80 x 40cm) of medium-weight
   fusible interfacing
32 x 16in (80 x 40cm) of heavyweight
   fusible interfacing
32 x 16in (80 x 40cm) of fusible fleece
About 3yd (2.75m) of 1in (25mm)-wide cotton webbing
Tape measure, ruler or set square
Pencil
Paper-cutting scissors
Pins
Dressmaking scissors
Sewing machine
Thread to match fabric
Iron and ironing board
Sewing needle
Thread for basting
Embroidery scissors

NOTE: The bag is sized to make the most of three contrasting fat quarters, with the minimum of wastage. You will need a whole fat quarter of the main fabric and the lining, but the gusset and pocket could be cut from leftovers.

Finished size is roughly:
8¾ x 12½ x 3in (22 x 32 x 7.5cm)

1 Use the templates on pages 134–5 to cut out the back and front of the bag from the main fabric. Cut two gusset pieces, each 15 x 4in (38 x 10cm), from contrast fabric. Fold the contrast fabric in half. Place the pocket template on the fold, then cut out a pocket. Cut a bag back and front, and a gusset from plain fabric as well.

2 Cut the medium-weight fusible interfacing, using the bag front and back template. Cut one pocket piece, folding the interfacing and placing the pattern piece on the fold. Also cut one piece measuring 28¾ x 4in (73 x 10cm), for the gusset.

3 Join two short ends of the two gusset pieces of the lining fabric with a ⅜in (1cm) seam. Press the seam flat. Using a hot iron, apply the interfacing to the wrong side of the gusset lining. Apply the interfacing to the wrong side of the back and front lining, and to the pocket.

4 Cut two pieces of heavyweight interfacing, using the bag front and back template. Apply this interfacing to the wrong side of the main fabric pieces, using a hot iron. Cut two pieces of fusible fleece, using the inner guideline on the template, and place this on top. Fuse in place using a hot iron.

5 Join the two gusset pieces in contrast fabric with a ⅜in (1cm) seam. Press the seam open. Cut a piece of heavyweight fusible interfacing 28¾ x 4in (73 x 10cm) and apply to the wrong side of the gusset. Cut a piece of fusible fleece 28 x 3⅛in (71 x 8cm) and place this on top. Fuse in place using a hot iron.

6 Fold the pocket in half along the foldline, with wrong sides together, and stitch around all the sides ³⁄₁₆in (5mm) from the edge. Pin the pocket to one of the main pieces (which will be the front of the bag), placing it centrally, with the lower raw edge lined up with the bottom edge of the bag. Baste by hand or machine down both sides and along the lower edge of the pocket, within the seam allowance.

7 Cut two 40in (1m) lengths of webbing. Pin and baste one piece to the front and one piece to the back of the bag, to form handles. Line up the ends with the bag base, and overlap the pocket on the front by ⅜in (1cm) with the inner edge of the webbing. Place a pin across the width of the webbing 2in (5cm) below the top edge of the bag. Topstitch close to the long edges and across the width at the points marked by the pins (see page 16). Remove the basting and topstitch again, ³⁄₁₆in (5mm) inside the first stitchline, to hold the straps firmly in place.

8 Pin the gusset to the front and back of the bag, easing the fabric around the corners. Baste, then stitch with a ½in (1.25cm) seam.

9 Snip into the seam allowance on the curved corners (see page 18).

10 Join the lining gusset to the lining back and front in the same way. Snip the seam allowance on the curved corners. Slip the lining inside the bag, with wrong sides together.

11 Line up the seams, then baste the top edges together by hand or machine. Fold the remaining webbing in half lengthways and use to bind the top edge (see page 18), pinning then basting in place. Topstitch close to the lower edge of the binding, and again ⅛in (3mm) above this stitchline.

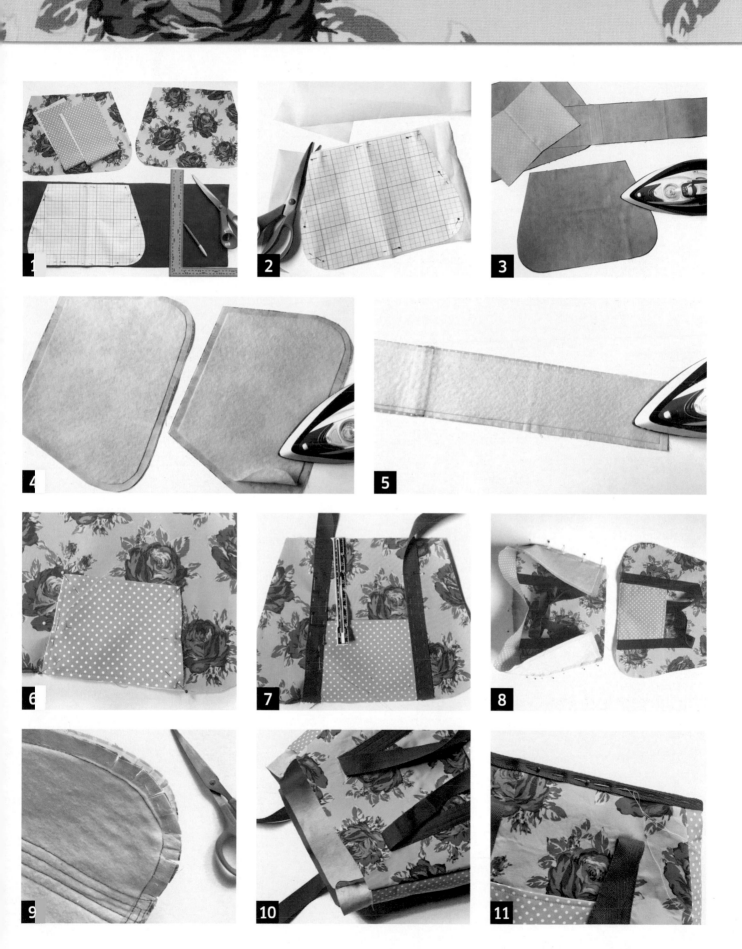

HOME
STORAGE

HANGING PODS

Hung from a hook, peg or doorknob, these little pods are ideal for tidying away all sorts of bits and pieces. Distribute them around the house: they will hold brushes and combs, wet wipes, cosmetics, clothes pegs, keys — the possibilities are endless.

Find the template on page 136

You will need
3 fat quarters in different fabrics
30 x 45in (76 x 114cm) of plain fabric, for lining
Pencil
Paper-cutting scissors
Tape measure or ruler
Pins
Dressmaking scissors
Sewing machine
Sewing needle
Thread for basting
Thread to match fabric
Iron and ironing board

Finished size is roughly:
16 x 7¾in (41 x 19.5cm)

NOTE: The seam allowance is ⅜in (1cm) throughout.

Tip
You can make three bags from one fat quarter. Choose co-ordinating prints that you can mix and match. The bags pictured here were made from the same design in three different colourways.

1 Use the template on page 136 to cut out a paper pattern. Fold each fat quarter in half. Stack them, with edges aligned. Pin the pattern in place and cut out. You will have two pieces of each design: a left and a right side. Cut six lining pieces from plain fabric, in the same way.

2 Pin and baste the top part of two fabric pieces to two lining pieces. Make sure you have one left and one right side of each. Stitch, beginning at the top and ending ⅜in (1cm) from the end of the seamline, as indicated on the pattern. This part will form the handle.

3 Remove the basting stitches and snip into the seam allowance on the curves (see page 18).

4 Open out each piece and press the seams towards the lining on either side. With right sides together, pin and baste the pieces of fabric together. While doing this, pin the handles out of the way so they don't get trapped in the seam.

5 Stitch, leaving a turning gap of about 4in (10cm) on the lower edge of the lining. Clip the corners and snip into the seam allowance on the curved edges.

6 Unpin the handles and turn the bag right sides out. Press. Tuck under ⅜in (1cm) on opening in lining, slipstitch the edges together (see page 15) and push the lining inside the bag.

7 Tuck under ⅜in (1cm) at each end of the handle and press, then slipstitch the edges together.

8 Topstitch (see page 16) either side of the join on the handle, and approximately ³⁄₁₆in (5mm) from the edge all around the handle and the top of the bag.

9 Pair the remaining fabric pieces and follow steps 1–8 to make two more bags.

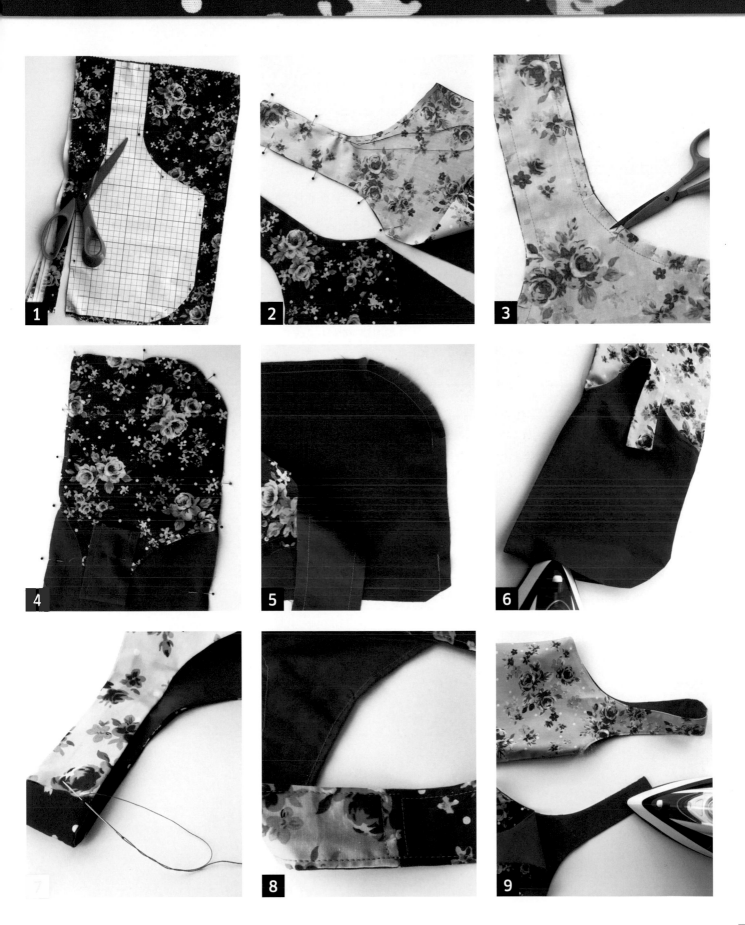

CLOTHES PROTECTOR

Designed to keep your favourite dress, jacket or suit clean and crease-free, this zipped cover makes a great addition to your wardrobe and can also be used to carry items of clothing on trips. Use a variety of printed fabrics or choose bold plain colours.

You will need
5 fat quarters of various fabrics
2¼yd (2m) of ⅝in (15mm)-wide plain bias binding
3½yd (3.25m) of ⅝in (15mm)-wide patterned bias binding
Lace-edged zip, about 48in (1.2m) long
Tailor's chalk or chalk pencil
Ruler
Pins
Dressmaking scissors
Sewing needle
Thread for basting
Thread to match fabric
Sewing machine with zipper foot
Iron and ironing board
Safety pin
Coat hanger

Finished size is roughly:
37 x 21in (94 x 53cm)

Tip
A lace-edged zip adds an extra level of detail to your project. Because it is decorative, there's no need to hide the zip when sewn.

1 Cut two 21¼ x 8¾in (54 x 22cm) rectangles from each fat quarter. You should have two sets of five different fabrics, one set for the front of the bag and one for the back.

2 Join five rectangles with French seams (see page 17). To do this, pin and baste the pieces with wrong sides together, aligning the long edges, and stitch with a ¼in (6mm) seam allowance. Open out the seams and press, then fold along the seamlines with right sides together, and stitch again, this time with a ⅝in (1cm) seam allowance. Open out, and press the seams to one side.

3 Choose one joined piece to be the front. Fold it in half lengthways and press, then open out and cut along the fold so you have two halves.

4 Cut the plain bias binding in half. Open out the binding and pin along the cut edge of one of the front pieces. Baste, then stitch along the foldline. Repeat with the other piece of fabric and binding.

5 Fold the binding to the wrong side along the seamline, so that no binding shows on the right side. Baste.

6 Lay this neatened edge along the wrong side of the zip; pin and baste in place. Do the same with the other half of the front.

7 Leave a small length of zip sticking out at either end, to be trimmed off later. Place a safety pin across the gap between the tapes, so that the slider does not slip off the end of the teeth.

8 On the right side, using a zipper foot, topstitch close to the zipper teeth on both sides (see page 16). Remove the basting stitches. Stitch a second row of topstitching, if necessary, to ensure that the zip is securely attached.

9 With wrong sides together, place the front of the bag on top of the back and pin together along the sides and lower edge. At the top, place the coat hanger on the bag and draw along the curved edge. Cut along the line you have drawn. At the bottom, place a saucer or similar round object on each of the two corners in turn, draw around the edge, then cut along the curved lines, to create rounded corners (see step 3, page 60).

10 Measure a gap on the top edge of about 4in (10cm), 2in (5cm) either side of the zip. Trim the front in a straight line between these points, trimming off the ends of the zip at the same time.

11 Use the patterned bias binding to bind the straight edge on the front, enclosing the end of the zip as you do so.

12 Baste all around, by hand or machine, close to the edge. When you come to the ends of the zip on the bottom edge, cut them off flush with the edge of the bag.

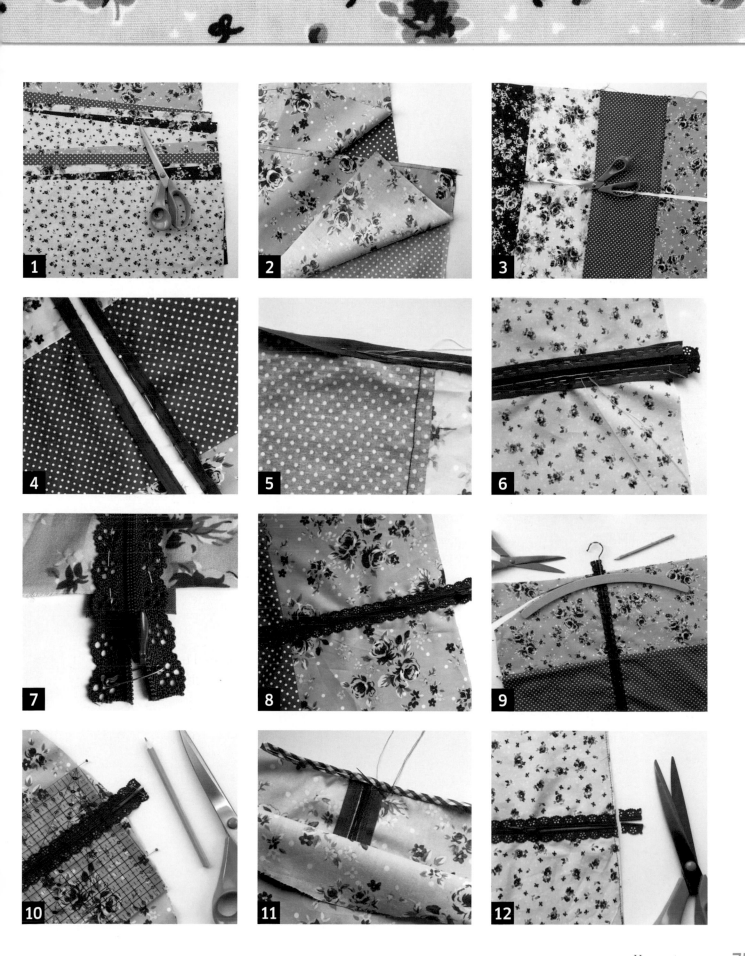

LARGE STORAGE BAG

This ample bag is useful for storing towels in the bathroom, bed linen or perhaps magazines and newspapers for recycling. The long handles are useful for carrying the bag and can be tucked away when not in use. The bag itself folds flat when empty.

You will need
5 fat quarters of various fabrics
$1\frac{1}{2}$yd (1.4m) of plain cotton fabric, for lining
50 x 45in (130 x 114cm) of heavyweight fusible interfacing
50 x 45in (130 x 114cm) of wadding
29 x $2\frac{1}{2}$in (73.5 x 6.5cm) of fusible fleece
60in (150cm) of 1in (25mm)-wide cotton herringbone twill tape
Tailor's chalk or chalk pencil
Ruler
Pins
Dressmaking scissors
Sewing machine
Sewing needle
Thread to match fabric
Thread for basting
Iron and ironing board

Finished size is roughly:
14 x 18½ x 14in (35.5 x 46 x 35.5cm)

1 From each fat quarter, cut four pieces. In total you will need 12 rectangles 10 x 8in (25 x 20cm) and eight squares 8 x 8in (20 x 20cm). From the remaining fabric, cut eight strips measuring 8 x 2½in (20 x 6.5cm).

2 Lay out the patchwork pieces until you are happy with the arrangement, then join the pieces in strips with a ⅜in (1cm) seam allowance.

3 Press all the seams open.

4 Pin the strips, right sides together, matching seams, then stitch. When joining short strips to longer ones, stitch as far as the seamline, leaving ⅜in (1cm) unstitched at the lower end. Press all seams open.

5 Open out the patchwork and use it as a template: cut one piece the same size of lining fabric, one of heavyweight fusible interfacing, and one of wadding.

6 On the interfacing, trim away ³⁄₁₆in (5mm) all round. Place it on the wrong side of the patchwork and fuse in place with a hot iron. Place the wadding on top, pin and baste, then machine stitch along the seamlines to quilt the layers together. Join the side seams on the bag: pin, baste and stitch with a ⅜in (1cm) seam. Do the same with the lining.

7 Join two sets of four strips to make two handles. Cut two strips of interfacing 29 x 1¼in (73.5 x 3cm); cut two strips the same size

of fusible fleece. Apply first the interfacing, then the fleece, down the wrong side of each patchwork strip.

8 Press the long edges to the wrong side, with the fold along the edge of the interfacing and fleece. Baste these edges. Then cut the cotton tape into two equal lengths and pin down the centre, covering the raw edges of the fabric. Baste, then stitch close to the edges of the tape.

9 Pin and baste the handles to the bag. To do this, line up the end of the handle with the raw edge at the top of the bag, on one of the short sides, positioning the handle halfway along one of the patchwork squares. Do the same with the other end of the handle.

10 Slip the lining inside the bag, with wrong sides together. Fold ⅜in (1cm) to the wrong side on both the bag and the lining, then pin the bag and the lining together, matching the seams. Baste the layers together, then slipstitch the lining to the outer bag (see page 15). Topstitch ³⁄₁₆in (5mm) from the top edge (see page 16) and again ¼in (6mm) from the first line of stitching.

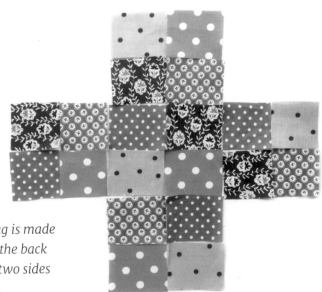

RIGHT: *The base of the bag is made from four rectangles; so is the back and the front. Each of the two sides is made from four squares.*

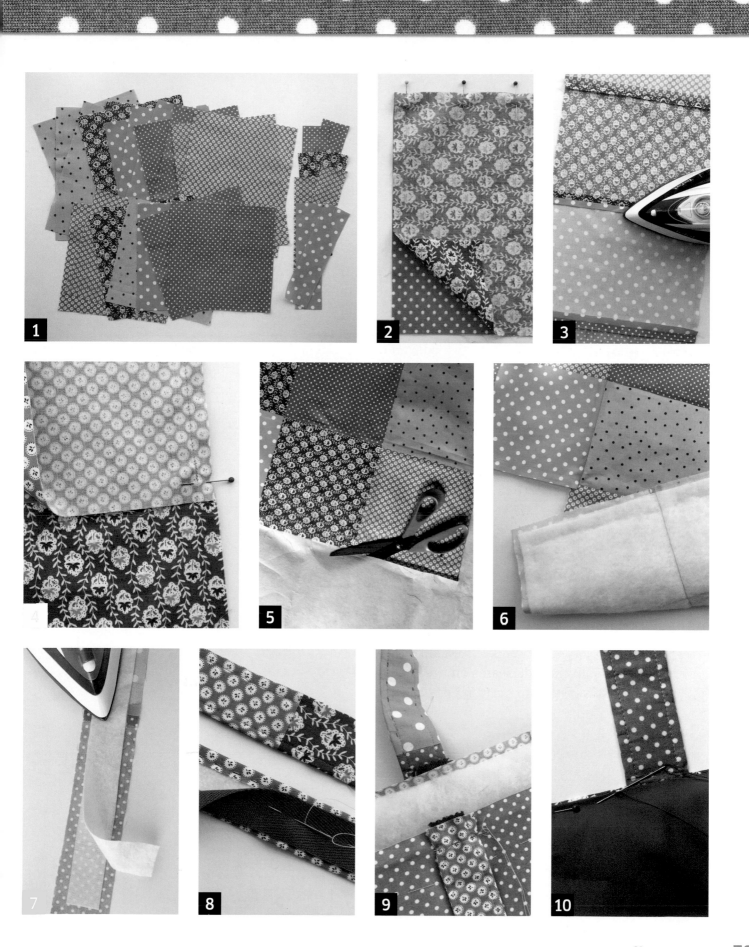

LINGERIE BAG

An envelope-shaped pouch is just the place to keep dainty items such as underwear, stockings and silk scarves. Make several and use them to organize your drawers. These flat pouches are also handy for packing small items for holidays.

Find the templates on pages
  136–7

You will need
1 fat quarter of main fabric
1 fat quarter of contrast fabric, for lining
About 22 x 12in (55 x 30cm) of fusible fleece
60in (1.5m) of lace-trimmed ½in (12mm)-wide
    double-fold bias binding
Pencil
Paper-cutting scissors
Pins
Dressmaking scissors
Iron and ironing board
Thick paper or thin card
Erasable pen or pencil
Tailor's chalk or chalk pencil
Ruler
Sewing machine
Sewing needle
Thread to match fabric
Thread for basting

Finished size is roughly:
8½ x 12in (21.5 x 30cm)

1 Use the bag template on page 137 to cut out a paper pattern, then cut one shape from each of the fat quarters and one from fusible fleece.

2 Trim ³/₁₆in (5mm) all round from the fleece, and apply it to the wrong side of the lining, using a hot iron.

3 Use the template on page 136 to draw a wavy line along a large piece of thick paper or thin card. Cut along the line to make a template, and use it to draw wavy lines, with an erasable pen or pencil, down the length of the main fabric piece.

4 Place the fabric pieces wrong sides together and baste through all layers, avoiding the wavy lines you have drawn. Machine sew along the wavy lines with a fairly long stitch length. Remove the basting stitches and erase any visible lines.

5 Press the work. Trim the edges to neaten them, if necessary. Bind the short straight edge with bias binding (see page 18), then lay the piece flat, with lining uppermost, and fold up 8in (20cm). Pin at each side.

6 Bind all around, except for the base, using the two-step binding method (see page 18). Begin on the right front, opening out the binding and matching the raw edge of the binding with the raw edges of the fabric. Backstitch along the foldline (or do this with your sewing machine). Slipstitch the folded edge of the binding to the back of the bag (see page 15).

7 Mark a ³/₄in (2cm) line in the centre of the flap, just above the binding, to make a buttonhole (see page 20).

8 Cut along the line. With two strands of embroidery thread, outline all round with a small running stitch, then complete the buttonhole with buttonhole stitch (see page 20).

9 Cover the button with matching fabric (see page 20). For a ³/₄in (2cm) button, you will need to cut a circle of fabric 1³/₈in (3.5cm) in diameter. Stitch the button to the bag, to correspond with the buttonhole.

Tip

The pictures show a hand-stitched buttonhole. Most modern sewing machines enable you to machine stitch a buttonhole, so you may prefer this option.

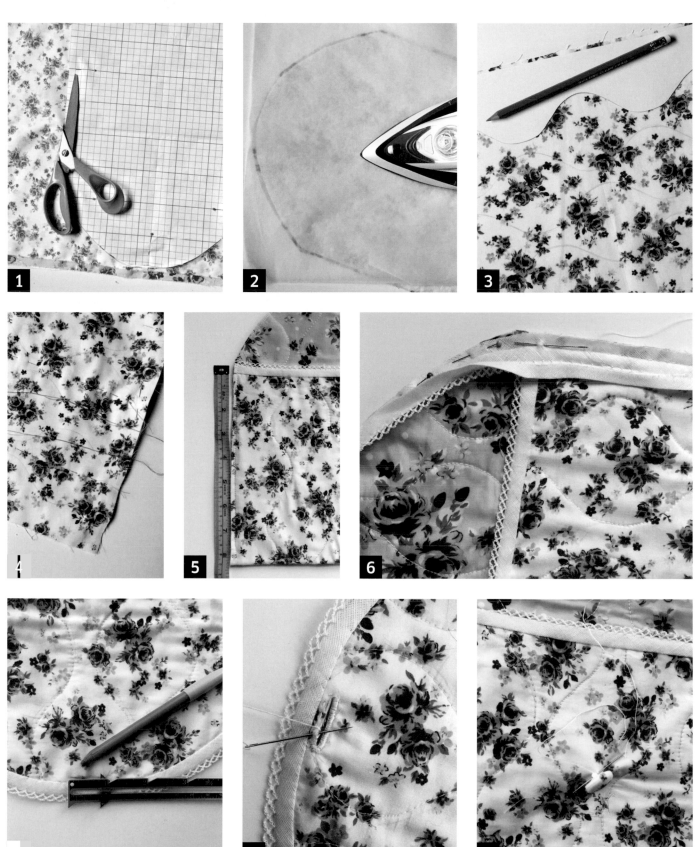

ART & CRAFT CADDY

It's helpful to keep all your craft essentials in one place. This practical carrier will hold large books and sketch pads, and has handy pockets ideally suited to craft items such as brushes, knitting needles and crochet hooks, as well as bulkier items such as craft glue. Knitters, stitchers and other hobbyists will wonder how they ever managed without it!

You will need
2 fat quarters of plain cotton canvas
2 fat quarters of printed cotton fabric, for lining
1 fat quarter of contrast printed cotton fabric, for exterior pockets
16½ x 14½in (42 x 36cm) of heavyweight fusible interfacing
13¾ x 6in (35 x 15cm) of buckram, for base
91in (2.3m) of 1in (25mm)-wide cotton herringbone twill tape
12in (30cm) of flat ¼in (6mm)-wide elastic
Tailor's chalk or chalk pencil
Pencil
Ruler
Set square (optional)
Pins
Clips (optional)
Dressmaking scissors
Iron and ironing board
Sewing machine
Sewing needle
Thread to match fabric
Thread for basting

Finished size is roughly:
9½ x 13½ x 6in (24 x 33.5 x 15cm)

NOTE: The dimensions of the pieces used to construct the bag are designed to make the most of the fat quarters, without too much wastage.

1 Place the two fat quarters of cotton canvas on top of one another and mark out rectangles of the following: 14½ x 10¾in (37 x 27cm) for the back and front; 14½ x 6¾in (37 x 17cm) for the base; and 10¾ x 6¾in (27 x 17cm) for the sides. Cut out. From a double layer of printed cotton, cut two pieces of these dimensions for the back and front lining, and the two sides.

2 From fusible interfacing, cut two pieces 14¼ x 10¼in (36 x 26cm) and two pieces 10¼ x 6¼in (26 x 16cm). Using a hot iron, apply the interfacing to the main pieces: back and front and two sides.

3 Pin the buckram centrally on one of the base pieces, and stitch in place all round.

4 Cut pockets from cotton fabrics. You will need two measuring 13¾ x 8in (35 x 20cm), four 8 x 4¾in (20 x 12cm) and two 8 x 6¾in (20 x 17cm).

5 On the two larger pockets, fold over ¼in (6mm) on one long edge to the wrong side and press. Fold over a further ½in (12mm) to create a hem. Stitch close to the bottom fold, to make a casing. On each of the four small pockets, fold over ¼in (6mm) and a further ½in (12mm), as before, to create hems. Topstitch (see page 16).

6 Place two small pocket pieces on the bag front, lining up the side edges and base. Baste in place. Insert a 5in (13cm) length of elastic in the top casing of one of the larger pockets and stitch the ends in place on either side. On the other long edge, stitch a gathering thread. Pin the side edges up against the edges of the smaller pockets and pull up the gathering threads until the bottom of the pocket fits the gap between the two smaller pockets.

7 Do the same on the bag back, with the two remaining small pockets and large pocket. Baste the side and bottom edges in place.

8 Cut two 45in (115cm) lengths of cotton tape. Pin one length of tape in place between the pockets on the bag front, then measure 2½in (6.5cm) from the top of the bag and mark with pins. Stitch the sides of the tape up to the marked point. Reinforce by stitching with a cross. Do the same with the other length of tape on the bag back.

9 Baste the medium-sized pockets to the sides of the bag, by hand or machine, lining up the side and bottom edges.

10 Stitch the bag sides to the front and back with a ⅜in (1cm) seam allowance: start the seams at the top and finish ⅜in (1cm) before you reach the lower edge. Do the same with the lining. Press seams open.

11 Pin, baste and stitch the bag base with buckram to the outer bag. Pin, baste and stitch the remaining base to the lining. Clip the corners (see page 18).

12 Turn under ⅜in (1cm) all round on the top edge of the bag outer and ½in (12mm) on the lining. Place the lining inside the bag, matching seams, and slipstitch the top of the lining to the inside of the bag (see page 15), positioning the lining just below the top edge of the bag. Topstitch all round.

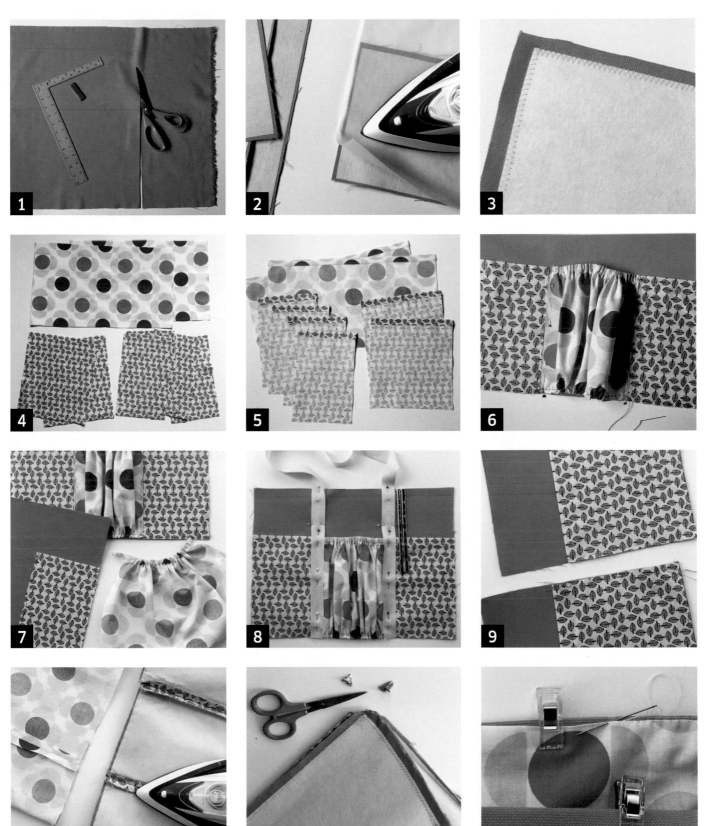

CHILDREN'S
BAGS

FOX PURSE

Cute, useful, and sure to impress, this little purse has a long shoulder strap so it won't get lost. The flap is easy to close with a press stud to keep those all-important special possessions secure when the proud owner is out and about.

Find the templates on pages 138–9

You will need
1 fat quarter of plain orange cotton
1 fat quarter of plain white cotton
1 fat quarter of printed cotton, for lining
Fusible fleece, at least 10¼ x 6¼in (26 x 16cm)
45in (115cm) of ⅜in (1cm)-wide velvet ribbon
45in (115cm) of ⅜in (1cm)-wide cotton herringbone twill tape
Black fabric-covered button, ½in (12mm) diameter, for the nose
Pencil
Paper-cutting scissors
Ruler
Pins
Dressmaker's chalk pencil
Erasable pen
Dressmaking scissors
Embroidery hoop
Iron and ironing board
Sewing machine
Sewing needle
Black embroidery silk
Thread to match fabric
Thread for basting
Press stud

Finished size is roughly:
4 x 5 (10 x 12.75cm), not including the shoulder strap

1 Cut a 6¼ x 5½in (16 x 14cm) rectangle from both plain orange and white fabrics, and a 10¼ x 6¼in (26.5 x 16cm) rectangle from the printed fabric. Using the templates on page 139, cut out the ears and snout from the orange and white fabrics.

2 Use the template on page 138 to trace the eyes and mouth on to the white rectangle with an erasable pen. Place the fabric in an embroidery hoop and embroider along the lines in split stitch (see page 15).

3 Join the orange and white fabrics – the back and front of the bag – along the base. Press the seam open.

4 Cut a 9¾ x 6in (24.5 x 15cm) rectangle of fusible fleece and apply to the wrong side of the joined pieces, using a hot iron. Using the paper template, cut snout and ear pieces from fusible fleece and trim away 3/16in (5mm) all around, then apply to the orange fabric pieces.

5 Fold the bag outer along the seam that joins the white and orange fabrics, and stitch the side seams with a 3/8in (1cm) seam allowance. Fold the lining in half, right sides facing, and stitch the side seams.

6 On the lower corners, align the side seam and base seam and press flat. From the corner, measure ½in (1.25cm) along the seam; with a pencil, draw a line across at right angles to the seam. Stitch along this marked line, then trim off the corners (see page 18). Do the same with the lining.

7 Pair the snout pieces and ears, and stitch together with a 3/8in (1cm) seam, leaving the lower edge unstitched. Trim the seam allowance.

8 Turn snout and ears right sides out and press.

9 On the top edge of the bag, turn ½in (1.25cm) to the inside and press. Baste. Pin the snout to the inside at centre back edge, lining up the raw edges. Pin the ears on either side. For the handle, stitch the velvet ribbon and tape together along both long edges and pin the ends next to the ears, on the seamline. Baste all pieces in place.

10 On the top edge of the lining, turn ½in (1.25cm) to the inside and press. Insert lining, pin in place, then slipstitch the top edge to the main purse (see page 15). Topstitch about 3/16in (5mm) from the top edge, all around (see page 16). Remove basting stitches.

11 Stitch one half of the press stud at the point of the snout, on the underside, and the other half at the top of the embroidered mouth. Stitch the covered button in place, on the top side of the snout, for a nose.

Tip

This small purse uses only a portion of the fabric. With three fat quarters – two plain and one patterned – you could make five or six of them.

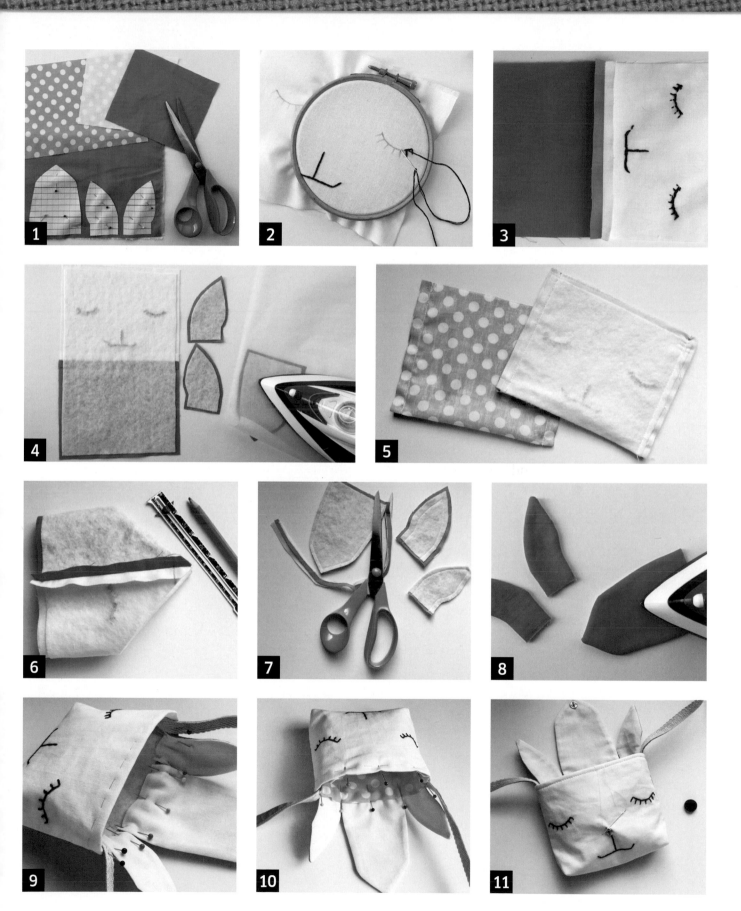

PARTY BAGS

Filled with toys and treats, these bags can be given to party guests as a lasting souvenir. Make them from fabric scraps, personalized with the recipient's initial for a special touch. With careful cutting, you will be able to make three party bags from two fat quarters.

Find the template on page 135

You will need

One fat quarter of main fabric

One fat quarter of contrast fabric, for lining

Scraps of cotton fabric, at least 2¾ x 2in (7 x 5cm), for each appliqué letter

Scraps of fusible bonding web, at least 2¾ x 2in (7 x 5cm), for each appliqué letter

3in (7.5cm) of cord elastic

Tape measure or ruler

Iron and ironing board

Pencil

Paper-cutting scissors

Dressmaking scissors

Tape measure or ruler

Pins

Sewing machine

Sewing needle

Thread to match fabric

⅝in (15mm) button with shank

NOTE: The seam allowance is ⅜in (1cm) throughout.

Finished size is roughly:
6 x 6 x 3¼in (15 x 15 x 8.5cm)

1 Using the template on page 135, cut the bag shape from the main and contrast fabrics. To do this, fold the fabric in half and press the fold, then place the pattern template on the fold, where indicated.

2 For the alphabet letter, find a template you like online and print out. Your letter needs to be about 2in (5cm) high so you may have to photocopy it at an increased or reduced size until you achieve this. Then trace your letter onto the paper backing of a piece of fusible bonding web. At this stage, the letter will be a mirror image. Place this on a scrap of fabric slightly larger than the bonding web and fuse in place using a hot iron, pressing for 10–20 seconds, according to the manufacturer's instructions.

3 Cut out the letter around the pencil line.

4 Peel off the backing paper and place the letter on the front of the bag, positioning the base approximately 2¼in (6cm) above the foldline. Press to fix in position.

5 Stitch around the letter, using a machine zigzag stitch. Set the machine's stitch length to 1 and the width to 2. You may like to practise on a spare fabric scrap first.

6 With right sides together, stitch the side seams on the main bag. Do the same with the lining. Press seams flat.

7 Open out each corner of the main bag and flatten, so that the end of the seam is in the centre. Press. Do the same with the lining.

8 Stitch across each corner on the main bag. Do the same with the lining.

9 Turn main bag right side out. Fold the cord elastic in half to form a loop, and stitch to the centre back of the bag.

10 Turn under a ³⁄₈in (1cm) hem; press. On the lining, turn under a ½in (1.25cm) hem.

11 Slip the lining inside the bag, wrong sides together, matching the side seams. Slipstitch the lining in place along the folded edges (see page 15).

12 Topstitch ³⁄₁₆in (5mm) from the top edge (see page 16). Stitch a button approximately 2in (5cm) from the top edge.

Tip

Instead of machine sewing around each letter, you can hand sew, using blanket stitch (see page 15).

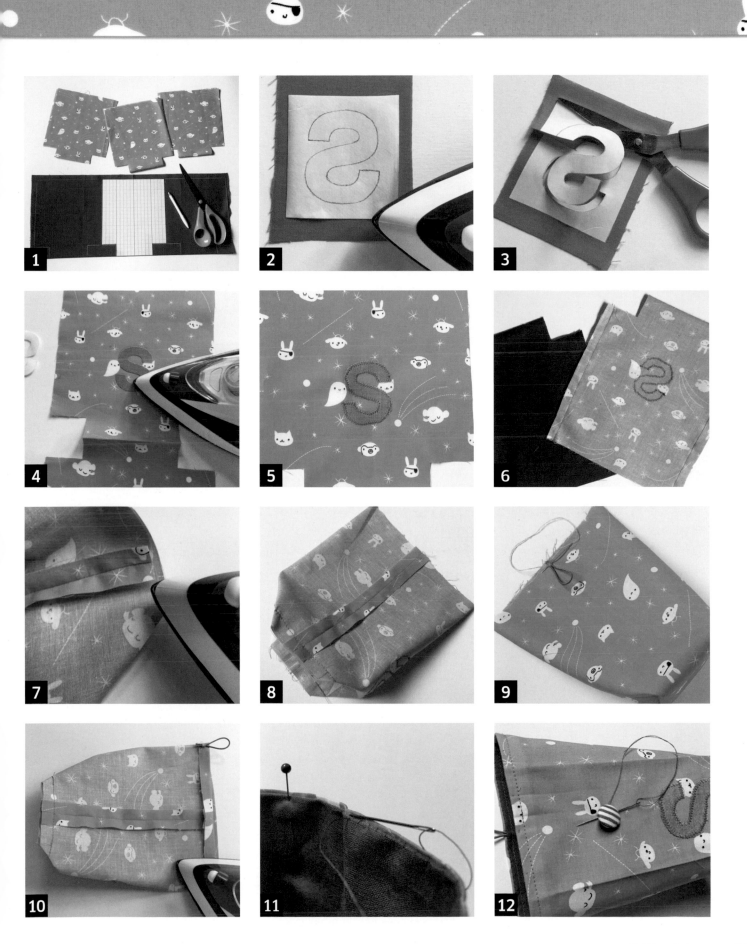

SWIMMING BAG

This lightweight backpack with a water-resistant lining has plenty of space for a towel, swimsuit and goggles, making it very practical. Choose a bright, eye-catching patterned fabric so that your bag is easily identifiable on the beach or at the pool.

You will need
2 fat quarters of main fabric
1 fat quarter of contrast plain fabric
About 16 x 30in (50 x 75cm) of ripstop nylon, for lining
6in (15cm) of 1in (25mm)-wide cotton tape
About 1yd (1m) of ½in (12mm)-wide bias binding
About 3yd (3m) of ¼in (6mm) piping cord
Pencil
Ruler
Tape measure
Pins
Dressmaking scissors
Sewing needle
Thread for basting
Sewing machine
Thread to match fabric
Iron and ironing board
Safety pin
Pinking shears (optional)

Tip
Ripstop nylon will help to make this bag tough, hardwearing, and fairly waterproof. It is sold in wide widths, and if you buy a full half yard (about half a metre), you will not use all of it for this project. Instead, you could look out for a remnant or perhaps reuse part of an old shower curtain.

Finished size is roughly:
16½ x 12½in (42 x 32cm)

1 Cut two 15¾ x 14¼in (40 x 36cm) rectangles of main fabric, being sure to make the shorter measurement across the width of the fabric, so that if there is a printed design, it is the right way up. Cut the same from nylon fabric. Cut two 14¼ x 5¼in (36 x 13cm) rectangles of plain fabric.

2 Place one of the plain strips right side up, and put a short edge of one of the main fabric pieces on top, lining up the edges. Place the nylon fabric on top, then pin, baste and stitch together with a ⅜in (1cm) seam. Repeat with the other three pieces of fabric. Press the seam towards the plain strip.

3 Pin the side seams, starting at the seam that joins the top strip and finishing ⅝in (1.5cm from the bottom edge. Cut two 3in (7.5cm) lengths of cotton tape. Fold each one in half and place between the fabric layers on either side of the bag, with ends protruding ¾in (2cm) above the lower edge of the bag.

4 Stitch the side seams with a ⅝in (1.5cm) seam allowance, finishing just below the tape loops, ⅝in (1.5cm) from lower edge of bag. Trim excess tape, using pinking shears if you have them.

5 Press the side seams open.

6 Turn under the raw edge of the seam allowance to meet the seam, tucking the ends of the tape under at the same time. Pin and topstitch (see page 16) from top to bottom, making sure the tape loop on the outside is not trapped in the stitching.

7 Stitch the seam at the base of the bag. Bind the raw edges of this seam with bias binding (see page 18).

8 Fold under and press ⅜in (1cm) on the top edges, then fold to the inside and slipstitch the fold to the seamline (see page 15).

9 With right side facing, topstitch ⅜in (1cm) from the base of the casing, then again ⅜in (1cm) from the top of the casing.

10 Cut the cord in half. Attach a safety pin to one end of one of the cords. Thread one length of cord through the channels and take the other end of the cord through the loop at the base of the bag. Knot the cord ends together. Repeat with the other length of cord, beginning and ending on the opposite side of the bag.

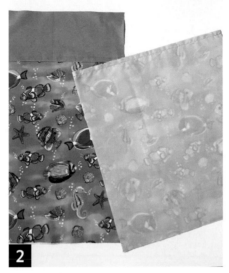

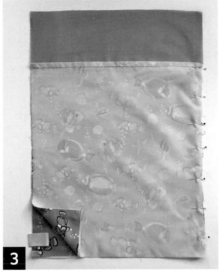

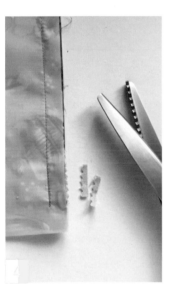

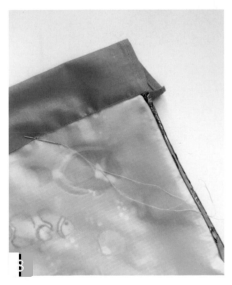

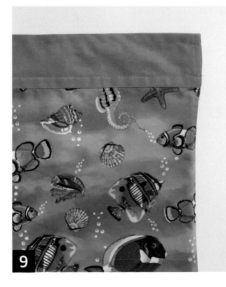

SLEEPOVER BAG

This zipped holdall is perfect for sleepovers at friends' houses, camping trips, or carrying sports kits. It's a good all-purpose bag. If you make it in a print to suit your child's interests, it is sure to become a firm favourite.

You will need
2 fat quarters of main fabric
1 fat quarter of contrast fabric
24in (60cm) of 44in (112cm)-wide plain cotton fabric, for lining
2yd (1.8m) of medium-weight fusible interfacing,
    29½in (75cm) wide
1¾yd (1.6m) of 1in (25mm)-wide cotton herringbone twill tape
18in (45cm) zip
Double-sided basting tape, ¼in (6mm) wide
Tailor's chalk or chalk pencil
Pencil
Ruler
Pins
Dressmaking scissors
Iron and ironing board
Sewing machine
Sewing needle
Thread to match fabric
Thread for basting

NOTE: The seam allowance is ⅜in (1cm) throughout.

Finished size is roughly:
7 x 13 x 7in (18 x 33 x 18cm)

1 Cut out two rectangles 14½ x 8in (36.5 x 20cm) from the main fabric and four from the lining fabric; cut two 8in (20cm) squares from the main fabric and two from the lining; cut two rectangles 16 x 4in (40.5 x 10cm) from main and two from the lining fabric.

2 From the fusible interfacing, cut six rectangles 14½ x 7¾in (36.5 x 19.5cm), four rectangles 15¾ x 3¾in (40 x 9.5cm) and four 7¾in (19.5cm) squares. Apply the interfacing with a hot iron to the wrong side of all main fabric and plain fabric pieces.

3 Cut two rectangles 10 x 5in (25 x 12.75cm) from the contrast fabric. Fold each one in half to make pockets, and topstitch ³⁄₁₆in (5mm) from the edge down both sides and across the fold (see page 16).

4 Place one pocket on each long side piece of the main fabric. Place the raw edge of the pocket along the bottom edge of the main fabric, and position it centrally.

5 Cut the tape in half, so you have two equal lengths of 31½in (80cm). Pin these to the sides of the bag, covering the pocket edges.

6 Pin the two square end pieces of main fabric to either end of one of the long side pieces. Baste, removing the pins as you go, then stitch.

7 Join one of the plain pieces, which will form the base of the bag, to the edge with the pocket base, then join the other side piece with the pocket to the other long edge of the base. Press the seams to one side.

8 Join the ends of the base to adjacent sides of each square end piece. Then join the ends of each side piece to the square ends of the bag. Make up the lining in the same way as the outer bag. On the top edge of both bag and lining, press ³⁄₈in (1cm) to the inside.

9 Pair the remaining rectangular pieces, placing right sides together, and stitch around two short sides and one long side. Clip the corners (see page 18), turn right sides out and press.

10 Apply double-sided basting tape along both stitched edges. Peel off the backing paper and press the zip in place, then topstitch on the right side, using a zipper foot.

11 Open the zip and insert the raw edge of the top pieces along the top edge of the bag. The top pieces will extend beyond the corner seams at each side. Pin, baste and stitch in place.

12 Pin the edges together at either end of the top, and topstitch the two pieces together, about ¼in (6mm) from the edge.

Tip

To hold the zip tapes in place before stitching, this project uses double-sided basting tape. Apply the tape where needed, place the zip on top, then stitch as usual. The tape remains sandwiched inside the zip tape and fabric. It shouldn't stick to the sewing machine needle, and can be laundered.

TOY SACK

Toys can be tidied away into this drawstring sack at the end of a play session and hung on a peg until the next time they're needed. You could make several in different fabrics; this type of bag is very simple to make and will always come in handy.

You will need
2 fat quarters of main fabric
1 fat quarter of contrast fabric
70in (1.8m) of ¼in (6mm) piping cord
Pencil
Tape measure or ruler
Pins
Dressmaking scissors
Sewing machine
Thread to match fabric
Embroidery scissors
Iron and ironing board
Sewing needle
Thread for basting
Safety pin

Finished size is roughly:
21 x 16in (53 x 41cm)

NOTE: Seam allowances vary throughout this project.

Tip
This bag is unlined, so you may wish to neaten seams on the inside; you will find methods for doing this on page 17.

1 Cut two 17¾ x 17in (45 x 43cm) rectangles of main fabric, being sure to make the shorter measurement across the width of the fabric, so that the design is the right way up. Cut two 17¾ x 10¾in (45 x 27cm) rectangles of contrast fabric.

2 Place the two main pieces, right sides together, and pin both layers together down the two long sides and across the base. Stitch with a ½in (1.25cm) seam allowance, then clip the corners with embroidery scissors. Remove the pins, turn right sides out and press.

3 On the two contrast pieces, which will form the wide border and casing at the top of the bag, fold ⅜in (1cm) to the wrong side on each short edge and press, then fold under a further ½in (1.25cm) to make a double hem, and press again. Check the length of each piece against the top of the bag to make sure they match, for a neat result. Adjust if necessary by re-folding and pressing again. Pin and stitch together.

4 On the right side of the bag, line up one long edge of one of the casing pieces with one top edge of the bag. Pin and baste. Do the same with the other casing piece, on the other side of the bag. Stitch ½in (1.25cm) from raw edges.

5 Press the seam allowance to one side, towards the casing. On the other long edge of the casing, fold ½in (1.25cm) to the wrong side and press.

6 Pin the folded edge of the casing to the inside of the bag, with the fold just covering the stitchline. Baste.

7 Turn right sides out and topstitch ⅛in (3mm) from the bottom edge of the casing all around (see page 16). Topstitch again, approximately ¼in (6mm) from the first line of stitching.

8 To form a channel, topstitch each casing again, 1in (2.5cm) from the previous line of topstitching. Cut the cord in half. Attach a safety pin to one end of one of the lengths and thread through the channels on both casings. Insert a second length from the opposite end of the channel so that you have two cord ends emerging at each side of the bag.

9 Cut two 6 x 3in (15 x 7.5cm) rectangles from offcuts of the main fabric. Fold each one in half with right sides together, and stitch the side seams ⅜in (1cm) from the raw edges. Clip the corners, turn right sides out and press.

10 On the open edge, fold ⅜in (1cm) to the inside and stitch a gathering (running) stitch by hand, around the top, close to the fold. Push the two ends of one of the cords into this little pocket, pull up the thread to gather, make a few stitches through the fabric and the cord, and fasten off securely. Do the same with the other pair of cord ends.

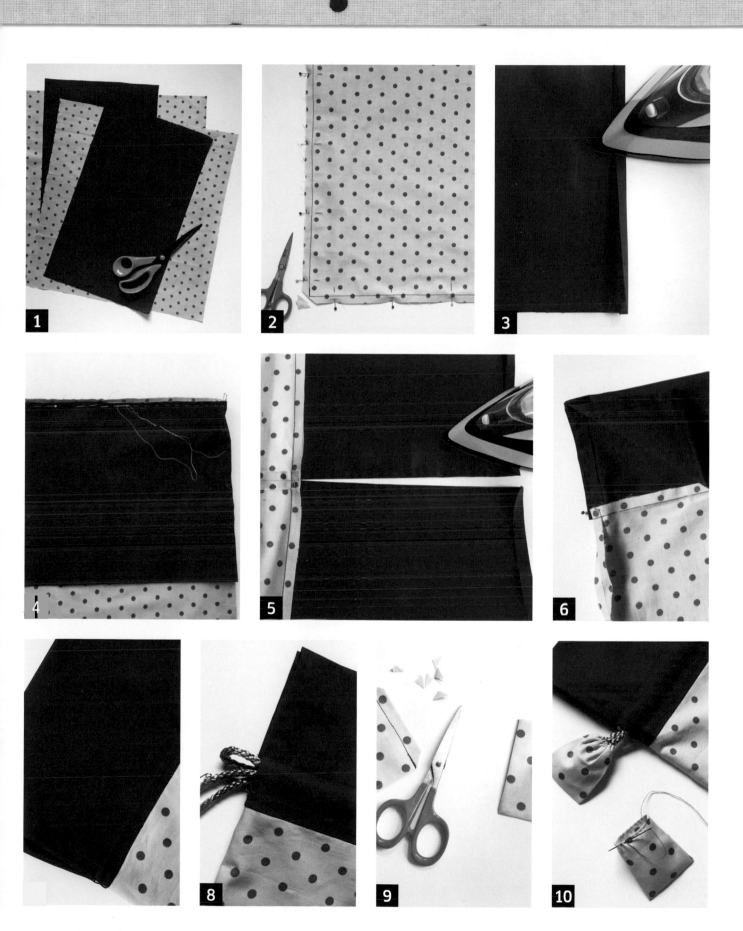

EVENING BAGS & PURSES

ENVELOPE CLUTCH BAG

Cute and quirky, lightly quilted, and edged with bobble braid, this clutch bag is suitable for all occasions and is surprisingly roomy. You will find it is large enough to accommodate your essentials for a night out: mobile phone, lipstick, keys and cash.

Find the templates on pages 140–1

You will need
1 fat quarter of main fabric
Remnant of contrast fabric, at least 12 x 5½in (30 x 14cm)
1 fat quarter of plain cotton fabric, for lining
15in (38cm) square of medium-weight fusible interfacing
15in (38cm) square of fusible fleece
Embroidery thread
¾in (2cm) magnetic closure
About 28in (70cm) of bobble braid
Pencil
Tailor's chalk
Paper-cutting scissors
Ruler or set square
Tape measure
Pins
Dressmaking scissors
Sewing machine with zipper foot
Sewing needle
Thread to match fabric
Iron and ironing board

Finished size is roughly:
10½ x 4½in (27 x 11cm)

1 Cut two rectangles measuring 11 x 4in (28x 10cm) from main fabric and one rectangle 11 x 5½in (28 x 14cm) from contrast. With the contrast fabric in the centre, join the three pieces with ³⁄₈in (1cm) seams. Press the seams open.

2 Place the pattern piece for the back and flap centrally on the joined piece and cut out. Cut out the bag front from main fabric.

3 Place the back and front right sides together, lining up the straight edge. Pin and baste together along this edge, then stitch with a ³⁄₈in (1cm) seam. Open out and press the seam flat.

4 Use the bag as a template to cut out one piece from fusible interfacing, one piece from fusible fleece and one piece from plain fabric.

5 Trim ³⁄₁₆in (5mm) all around the interfacing and use a hot iron to fuse it to the wrong side of the lining.

6 Trim ⁵⁄₁₆in (8mm) all around the fusible fleece and fuse to the wrong side of the main piece.

7 Attach one half of the magnetic closure (the one with the knob) to the lining flap, as indicated on the pattern template. Attach the other half of the magnetic closure (the one with the indentation) to the front of the bag.

8 With a single strand of embroidery thread, stitch outlines of running stitch around areas of the printed design, to create a quilted effect.

9 Place the main piece and lining right sides together. Pin and baste all round, then stitch with a ³⁄₈in (1cm) seam, leaving an opening of about 4in (10cm) on the long edge, for turning. Snip into the seam allowance on curves (see page 18). Turn right sides out through the opening. Press under ³⁄₈in (1cm) on the open edge and slipstitch the folded edges together, to close.

10 Pin bobble braid around the edge, starting and ending at the seamline. Machine stitch the braid in place, removing pins as you go.

11 Fold up the lower part along the seamline, to form the front of the bag. Slipstitch the edges together (see page 15), catching the folded edge of the lining only with the tip of the needle, then topstitch all around the sides and the edge of the flap (see page 16).

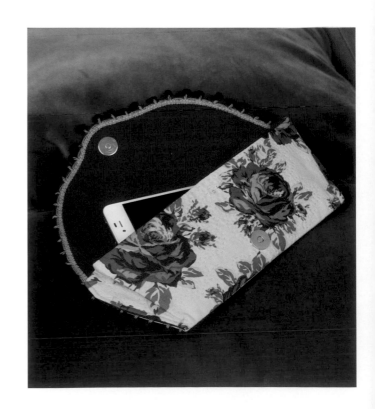

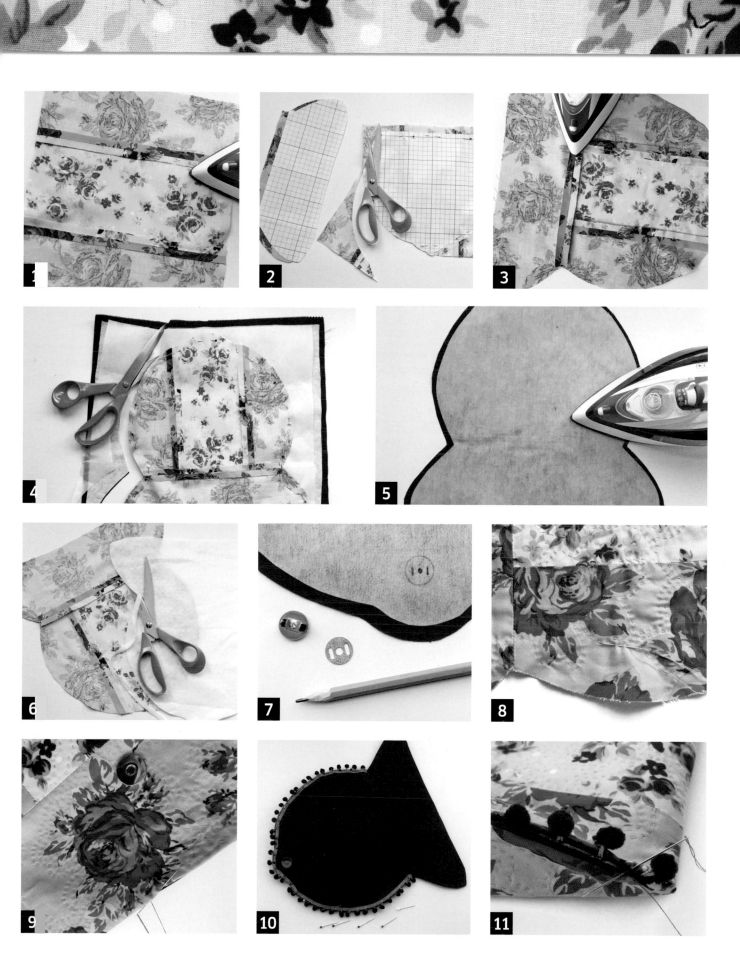

MAKE-UP BAG

Just big enough for a few essential items such as a lipstick, perfume atomizer and some tissues, this dinky make-up bag will take up very little room in your handbag. Despite its tiny size, it is a practical item, with a waterproof lining.

You will need
1 fat quarter of fabric
12 x 8in (30 x 20cm) of 12-gauge clear vinyl fabric
7in (18cm) zip with metal teeth
Tape measure
Pencil
Dressmaking scissors
Pins
Sewing needle
Thread for basting
Sewing machine with zipper foot
Thread to match fabric
Ruler or set square
Iron and ironing board
Pinking shears (optional)

NOTE: The seam allowance is $5/8$in (1.5cm), except for the zip.

Finished size is roughly:
$3^{1}/_{2}$ x $3^{1}/_{2}$ x $2^{1}/_{2}$in (9 x 9 x 6.5cm)

1 Cut a rectangle of fabric measuring 12 x 8in (30 x 20cm). Place the fabric on top of the vinyl, matching the edges, and baste the layers together all round, within the seam allowance.

2 Place the zip face down along one short edge of the right side of the fabric, and baste in place. Fit a zipper foot to the sewing machine and stitch down the centre of the zip tape.

3 Fold back the top edge of all three fabrics (the lining, the main fabric and the zip tape) by ³⁄₈in (1cm). Then topstitch ¹⁄₈in (3mm) from the fold (see page 16).

4 With right sides together, fold the fabric in half. Align the short edge of the fabric with the unstitched edge of the zip tape, baste and machine stitch together. Then topstitch on the right side of the fabric, as in step 3. Open the zip in order to do this.

5 Do up the zip about halfway, turn the fabric inside out and flatten, with the zip in the centre. At the top end, hand stitch the edges of the zip tape together to prevent them from splaying out. Leave a small gap between the tapes instead of pulling tight – otherwise, you will distort the zip.

6 Pin and machine stitch the seam across each end, ⁵⁄₈in (1.5cm) from the edges.

7 Measure and mark a rectangle 1³⁄₄ x 1¹⁄₄in (4.5 x 3cm) on each corner. Take the smaller measurement from the folded edge and the larger measurement from the seamed end, as shown.

8 Cut along the lines you have drawn.

9 Open out each corner and flatten, so that the straight edges align and the seam is in the centre. Pin and baste these edges together, then machine stitch.

10 Press the seam to one side, away from the zip. Stitch each corner seam and trim, using pinking shears if you have them. Turn the bag right side out through the opening in the zip.

Tip

It is very tricky to machine sew small items. If you open the zip, this will help you to sew it in, or you could backstitch by hand instead.

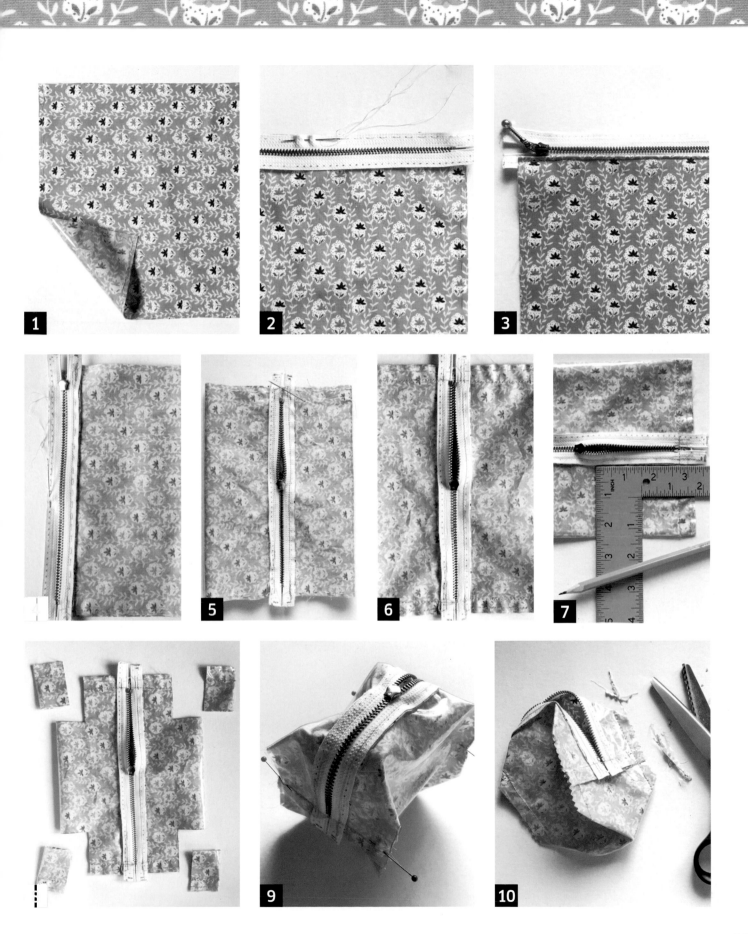

POWDER-COMPACT PURSE

This purse is designed to hold a round, square or rectangular powder compact or a pocket-sized mirror measuring up to 3¾in (9.5cm) across. Made with a luxurious silk lining and satin bias binding, it is just the thing for a special evening out.

Find the template on page 140

You will need
1 fat quarter of main fabric
12 x 5in (30 x 12cm) of silk fabric, for lining
12 x 5in (30 x 12cm) of wadding
26in (66cm) of ½in (12mm)-wide satin bias binding
1 decorative button
Pencil
Paper-cutting scissors
Ruler or set square
Tape measure
Pins
Dressmaking scissors
Sewing machine
Sewing needle
Thread to match fabric
Embroidery thread for quilting, in matching or contrast colour
Iron and ironing board

NOTE: You can quilt freehand, following the printed design on your fabric, or draw lines to follow with an erasable pen or pencil. Sew lines of running stitch using a matching or contrasting thread to achieve different effects.

Finished size is roughly:
4 x 4½in (10 x 11.5cm)

1 Using the template on page 140, cut one piece each of main fabric, wadding and lining.

2 Sandwich the wadding between the main fabric and lining, and baste all around.

3 Thread a needle with a single strand of embroidery thread and sew lines of running stitch along the length of the piece, taking the needle through all layers.

4 Cut a 6in (15cm) length of binding, open it out and pin to the short concave edge. Remove the basting stitches from this edge. Backstitch along the foldline, through all layers, removing the pins as you go.

5 Fold the binding over so that the folded edge just covers the stitchline. Pin, then slipstitch the folded edge in place (see page 15).

6 Trim off excess binding at each end and remove the remaining basting stitches.

7 Fold up the lower edge and pin to create a pocket 3¾in (9.5cm) up from the fold. Stitch the sides of the pocket together, close to the edges.

8 Cut a 20in (51cm) length of bias binding, open it out and pin all round the purse, apart from the lower edge. Backstitch along the foldline, through all layers.

9 Fold over and slipstitch the folded edge of the binding to the stitchline, as before, tucking raw ends under neatly.

10 Mark a ¾in (2cm) buttonhole, 1in (2.5cm) up from the edge of the flap. Stitch around the buttonhole, close to the marked line, in running stitch, then cut through all layers and work buttonhole stitch all around (see page 20).

11 Sew a button in place on the front, to correspond with the buttonhole.

Tip

You could use a press stud instead of sewing a buttonhole. To cover a press stud, cut circles of fabric 1¼in (3cm) in diameter and follow the instructions on page 20.

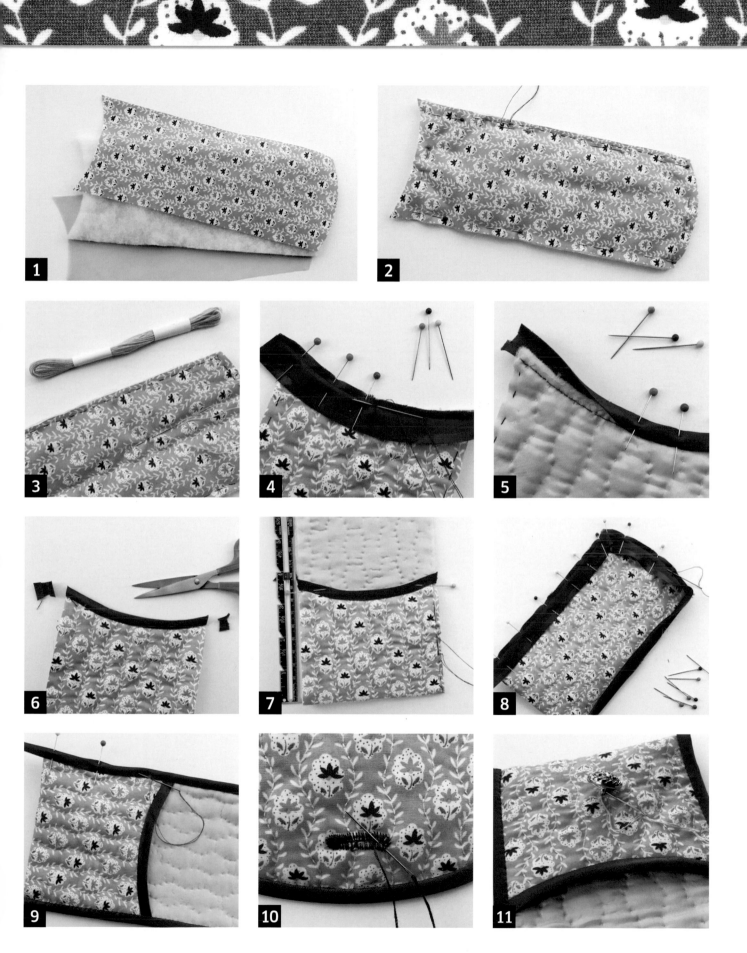

LIPSTICK POUCH

Stitch this little drawstring pouch to carry around your favourite lipstick. Combined with a mirror in a matching case, it makes a lovely small gift. If you're not a lipstick wearer, the drawstring pouch would also make a handy home for your earphones.

You will need
1 fat quarter of main fabric
1 fat quarter of plain cotton fabric, for lining
10 x 8in (25 x 20cm) of medium-weight fusible interfacing
12in (30cm) of 1in (25mm)-wide ribbon
1yd (90cm) of ¼in (6mm)-wide ribbon
2 pompoms (see note)
Mirror, approximately 3¼ x 2¼in (8.25 x 5.5cm)
Ruler or set square
Tape measure
Pins
Dressmaking scissors
Sewing machine
Sewing needle
Thread to match fabric
Iron and ironing board
Fabric glue

Finished size is roughly:
6 x 4in (15 x 10cm) for the pouch;
4½ x 3½in (11.5 x 9cm) for the
matching case

NOTE: For the little pompoms, simply cut off two bobbles from a length of purchased braid.

Tip
From two fat quarters you could make four of these pouches – or if you only wish to make one, you could use small pieces of fabric left over from other projects.

1 Cut a rectangle measuring 12⅝ x 4¾in (32 x 12cm) from both the main and lining fabrics.

2 With right sides together, join the pieces along both short edges with a ⅜in (1cm) seam. Press the seams open.

3 Align the seams and stitch along the long edges, leaving a turning gap in the lining of approximately 2⅜in (6cm).

4 Turn right sides out, turn under ⅜in (1cm) on opening, and slipstitch closed (see page 15). Push the lining inside the bag.

5 Cut two 4¾in (12cm) lengths of the wider ribbon and press under ⅜in (1cm) at each end. Stitch across the ends.

6 Pin the ribbon pieces to the top of the bag, one on each side, and stitch in place, leaving the ends open, to form a casing.

7 Cut two 15¾in (40cm) lengths of narrow ribbon and thread them through the ribbon casing, one from either end. Stitch the ends together and attach a pompom.

8 To make the matching case for the mirror, draw two rectangles 3¾ x 4¾in (9.5 x 12cm) onto the fusible interfacing. Inside one of these pieces of interfacing, draw a smaller rectangle 1¾ x 2¾in (4.5 x 7.5cm). Fuse the interfacing to the wrong side of the leftover piece of main fabric, taking into consideration the motifs on the fabric when positioning it. Make sure the two parts of the frame are at least 1in (2.5cm) apart, so there is room for the seam allowance. Draw a line on the fabric ⅜in (1cm) outside the frame outline, for the seam allowance.

9 Cut out the two pieces of the frame along the outer lines. Then cut along the lines within the frame, to create an aperture on the frame front. Fold the fabric back along these lines.

10 On the right side of the fabric, topstitch all round (see page 16), 3/16in (5mm) from the inner edge of the frame.

11 Place the front and back, right sides together, and stitch all round with a ⅝in (1.5cm) seam allowance. Clip the corners and trim the seams to reduce bulk (see page 18).

12 Turn right sides out and press. Place the mirror inside the frame, apply fabric glue to the edges and place a weight on top until the glue is dry.

CLIP-FRAME EVENING BAG

Simple but sophisticated, with a secure metal frame clasp and elegant shoestring straps, this bag is suitable for most occasions. Choose a fabric to match or contrast with your favourite outfit – or why not make a few to go with different outfits?

You will need
1 fat quarter of main fabric
1 fat quarter of plain linen, for lining
51 x 45in (130 x 114cm) of fusible fleece
Metal frame clasp
Bespoke template, based on your clasp
40in (1m) of piping cord
Paper (plain, or with grid)
Pen or pencil
Ruler or set square
Paper-cutting scissors
Tape measure
Pins
Dressmaking scissors
Iron and ironing board
Sewing machine
Sewing needle
Thread to match fabric
Thread for basting
Loop turner
Safety pin
Knitting needle or similar for poking out corners

Finished size is roughly:
6 x 9½in (15 x 24cm)

NOTE: The seam allowance is ⅜in (1cm), unless otherwise stated.

1 Place the clasp on the paper and draw around the outside edge. Hold the top corner of one end of the clasp, swivel the hinged end outwards ¾in (2cm) and make a mark on the paper. Then draw a line from the top corner to this mark. Repeat on the other side.

2 From the ¾in (2cm) mark, draw a line at a slight angle downwards, for the side of the bag, and a line across the bottom for the base. Mark a point (X) in line with each hinge, ⅜in (1cm) from the outer edge.

3 To make sure the pattern is symmetrical, fold it in half and trim it, if necessary. Use this template to cut out two pieces from the main fabric and two pieces from the lining. Transfer the marked points (X) to the fabric pieces.

4 Using the same pattern, cut two pieces of fusible fleece and trim away ¼in (6mm) all round. Apply the fleece to the wrong side of each of the main bag pieces.

5 Place the main bag pieces right sides together. Pin, baste and stitch the sides and base of the bag with a ⅜in (1cm) seam, starting and ending at the marked points. Do the same with the lining but leave a 4in (10cm) turning gap in the seam in the centre of the base.

6 Align the base and side seams on each corner. Measure ⅝in (1.5cm) from the corner and stitch across at this point. Trim off excess fabric. Do the same with the lining.

Tip
You can make the lower part of the bag any shape you like – rounded, square or rectangular, for example.

7 Slip the lining inside the bag, with right sides together. Stitch the lining to the main bag, all round the top edge, starting and finishing at the marked points. Snip into the seam allowance on the curves (see page 18) and trim away some of the seam allowance to reduce bulk.

8 Turn the bag right sides out through the gap in the lining. Use a knitting needle or similar object to poke out the corners.

9 On the opening, turn under ⅜in (1cm) to inside and slipstitch the folded edges together (see page 15).

10 Press the two top sections of the purse. With the metal clasp open, push these sections into the two halves of the clasp, using the tips of your scissors to help you push the fabric into the metal grooves.

11 Stitch the fabric to the clasp by inserting the needle into each of the clasp holes in turn. Depending on the type of clasp you are using, you can choose to use a running stitch or backstitch, or oversewing. In this case, there are two rows of holes, both of which can be used.

12 To make the strap, cut two strips of main fabric 21¼ x 1³⁄₁₆in (54 x 3cm). Join them together with a ¼in (6mm) seam, to make one long strip. Fold it in half lengthways and stitch down the length with a ¼in (6mm) seam, then turn right sides out using a loop turner (see page 21). Attach a safety pin to one end of the length of cord and thread through this fabric tube. Using the tips of your scissors, tuck in the raw edges of the fabric at each end. Thread each end of the strap through a ring on the top of the clasp, double back in a loop and stitch the end firmly in place.

TEMPLATES

Templates that are shown at actual size can be traced and cut out, or photocopied. For templates that have been reduced in size, enlarge them on an A3 photocopier to the percentage stated.

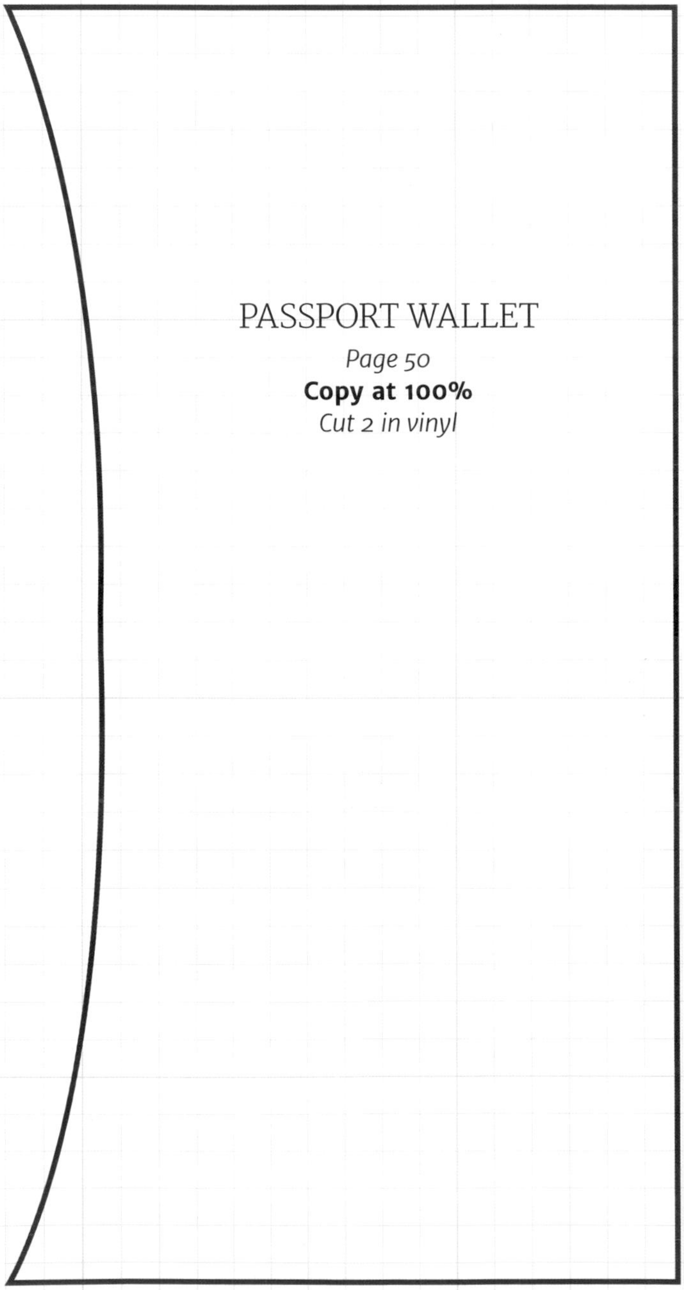

PASSPORT WALLET
Page 50
Copy at 100%
Cut 2 in vinyl

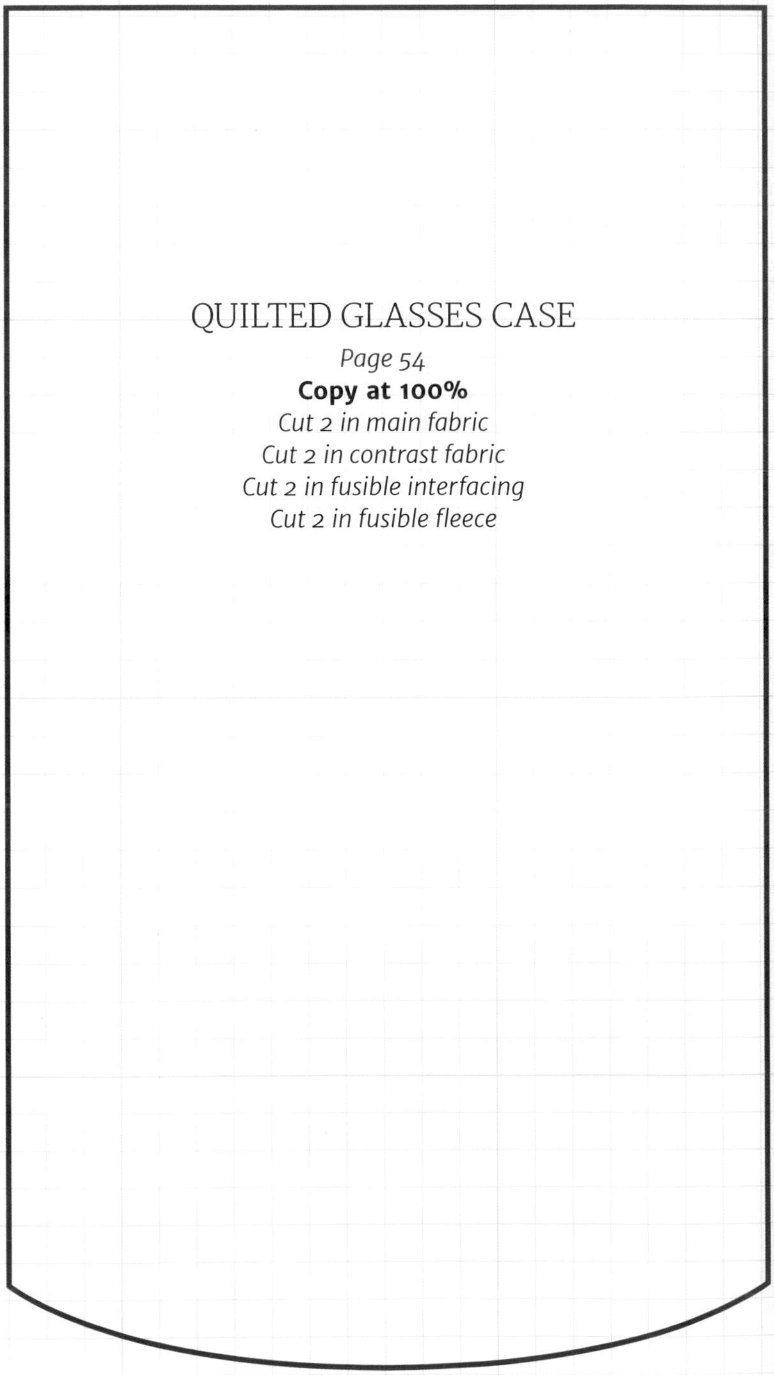

QUILTED GLASSES CASE
Page 54
Copy at 100%
Cut 2 in main fabric
Cut 2 in contrast fabric
Cut 2 in fusible interfacing
Cut 2 in fusible fleece

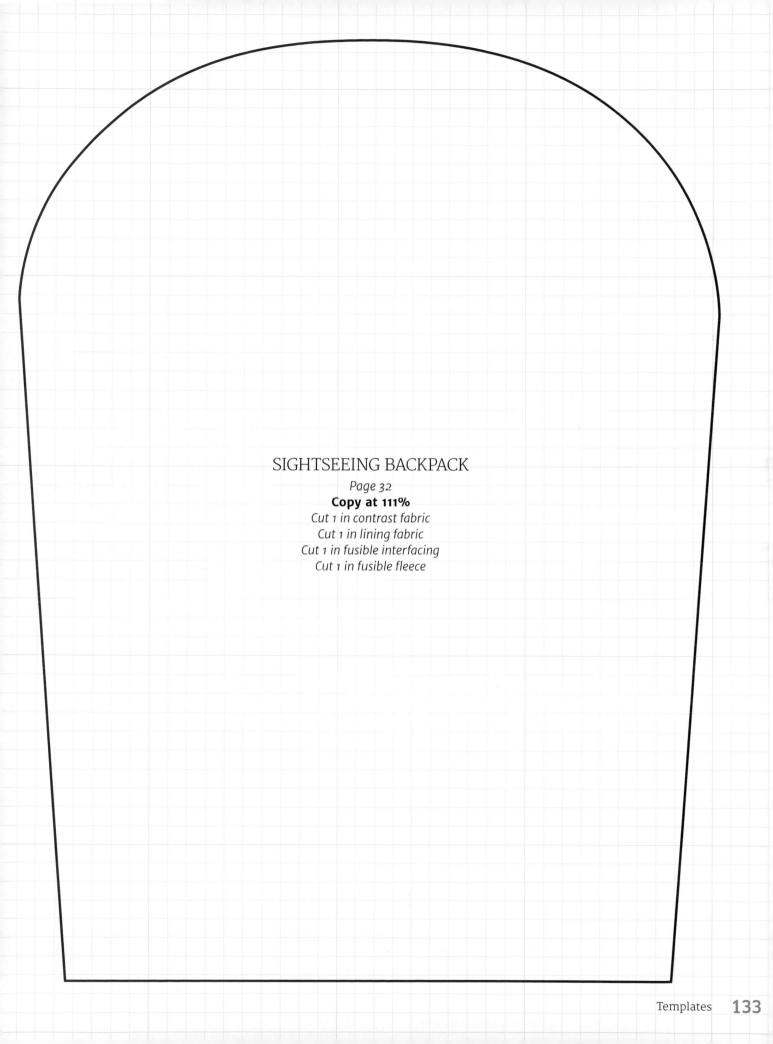

SIGHTSEEING BACKPACK

Page 32
Copy at 111%
Cut 1 in contrast fabric
Cut 1 in lining fabric
Cut 1 in fusible interfacing
Cut 1 in fusible fleece

SHOULDER BAG
BACK AND FRONT
Page 62
Copy at 133%
Cut 2 in main fabric
Cut 2 in medium-weight
fusible interfacing
Cut 2 in heavyweight
fusible interfacing
Cut 2 in fusible fleece

3/8 in (1cm) seam allowance

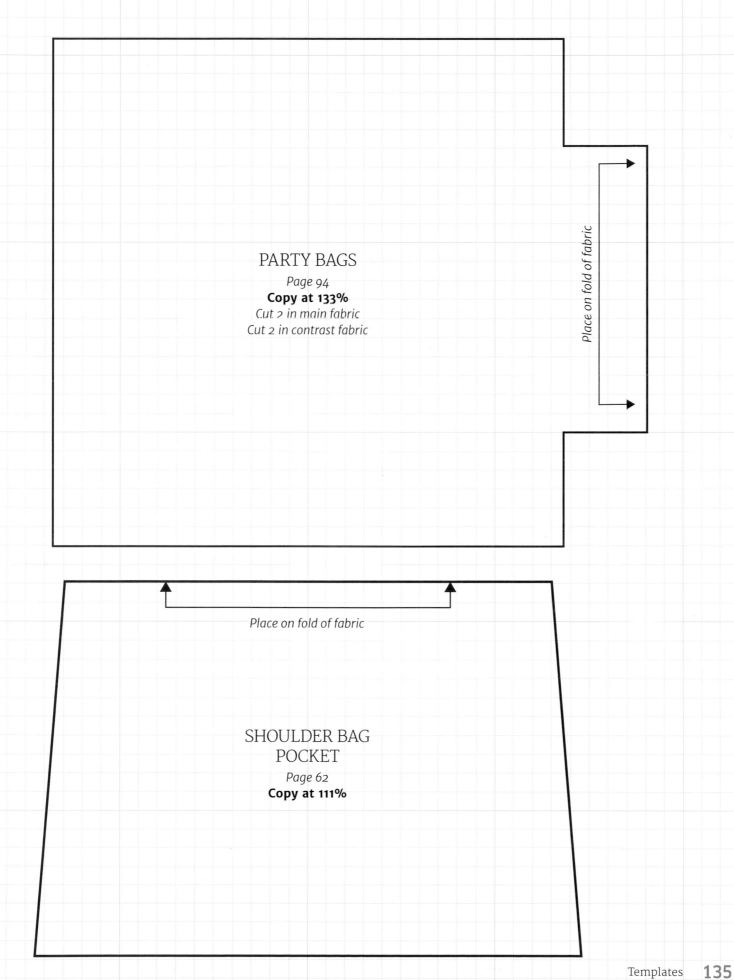

PARTY BAGS

Page 94
Copy at 133%
Cut 2 in main fabric
Cut 2 in contrast fabric

Place on fold of fabric

Place on fold of fabric

SHOULDER BAG
POCKET

Page 62
Copy at 111%

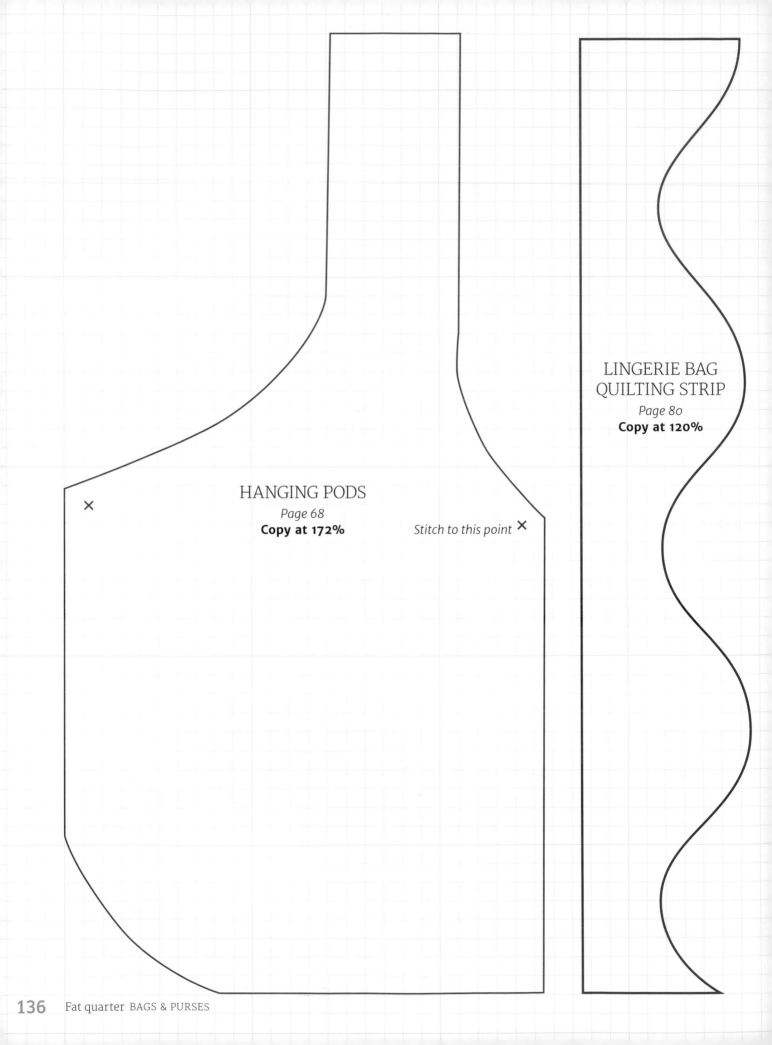

HANGING PODS

Page 68
Copy at 172%

Stitch to this point ✕

✕

LINGERIE BAG
QUILTING STRIP

Page 80
Copy at 120%

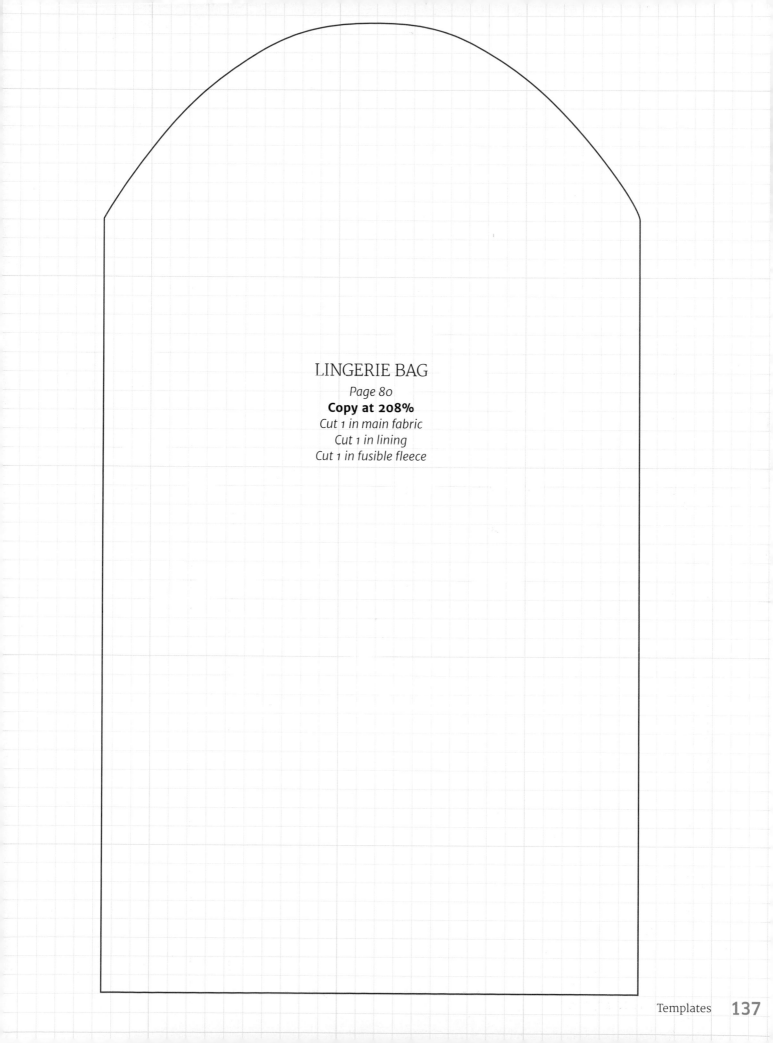

LINGERIE BAG

Page 80
Copy at 208%
Cut 1 in main fabric
Cut 1 in lining
Cut 1 in fusible fleece

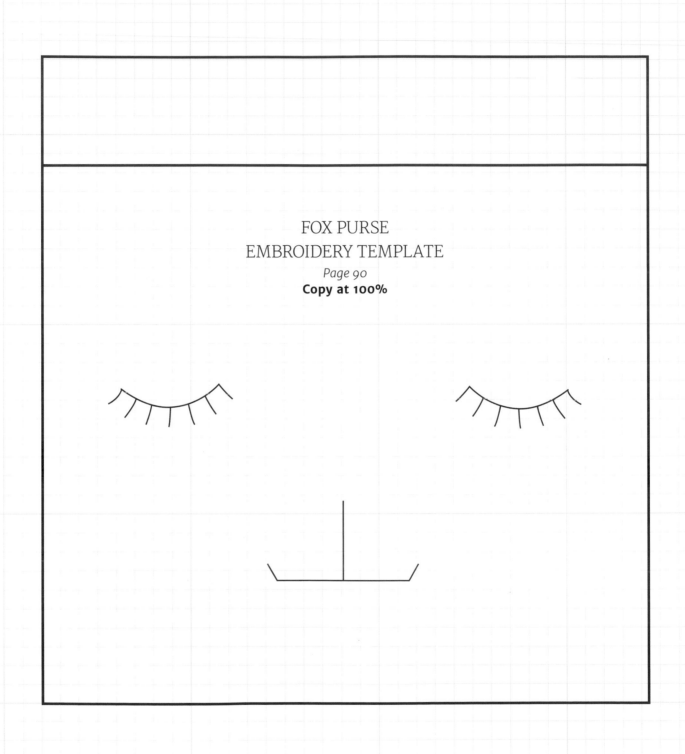

FOX PURSE
EMBROIDERY TEMPLATE
Page 90
Copy at 100%

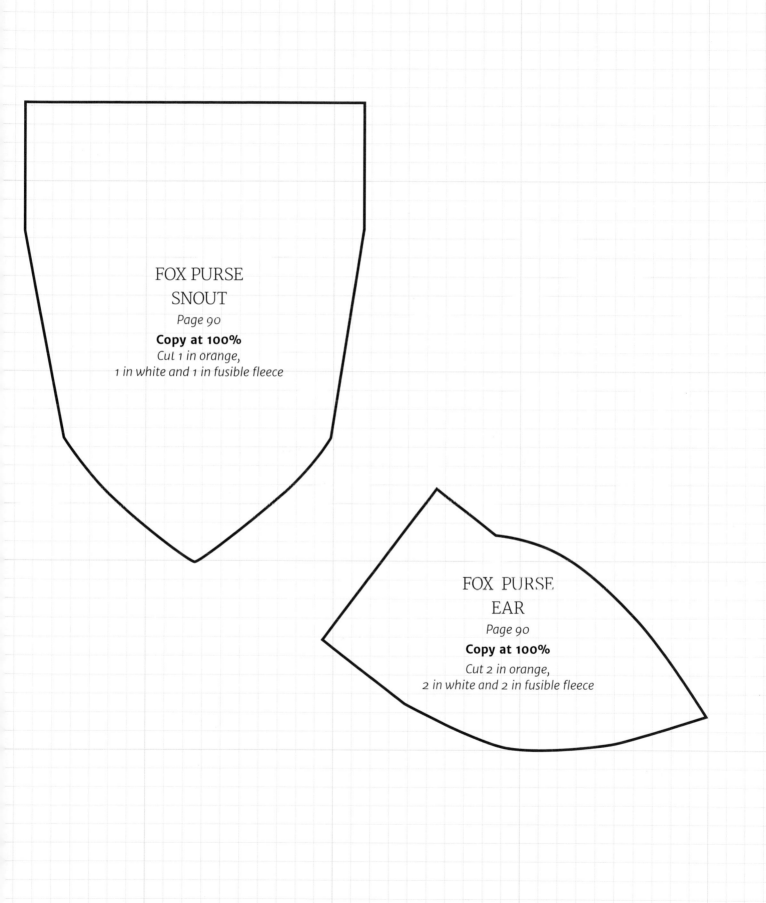

FOX PURSE
SNOUT

Page 90

Copy at 100%
*Cut 1 in orange,
1 in white and 1 in fusible fleece*

FOX PURSE
EAR

Page 90

Copy at 100%

*Cut 2 in orange,
2 in white and 2 in fusible fleece*

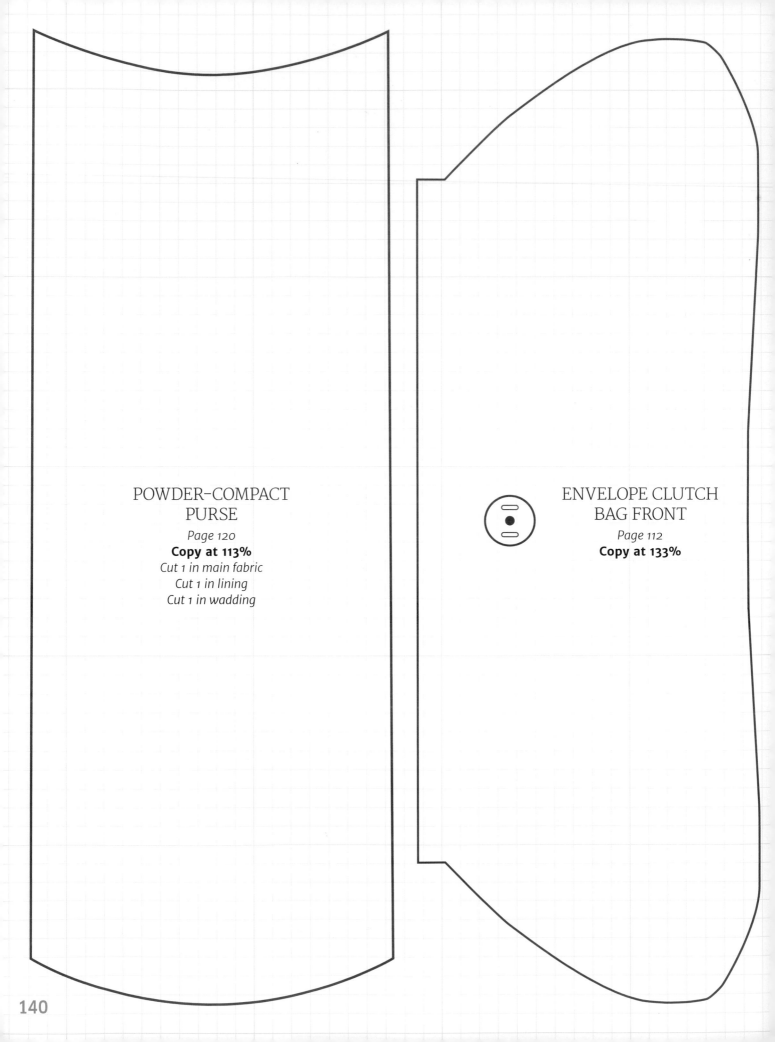

POWDER–COMPACT
PURSE

Page 120
Copy at 113%
Cut 1 in main fabric
Cut 1 in lining
Cut 1 in wadding

ENVELOPE CLUTCH
BAG FRONT

Page 112
Copy at 133%

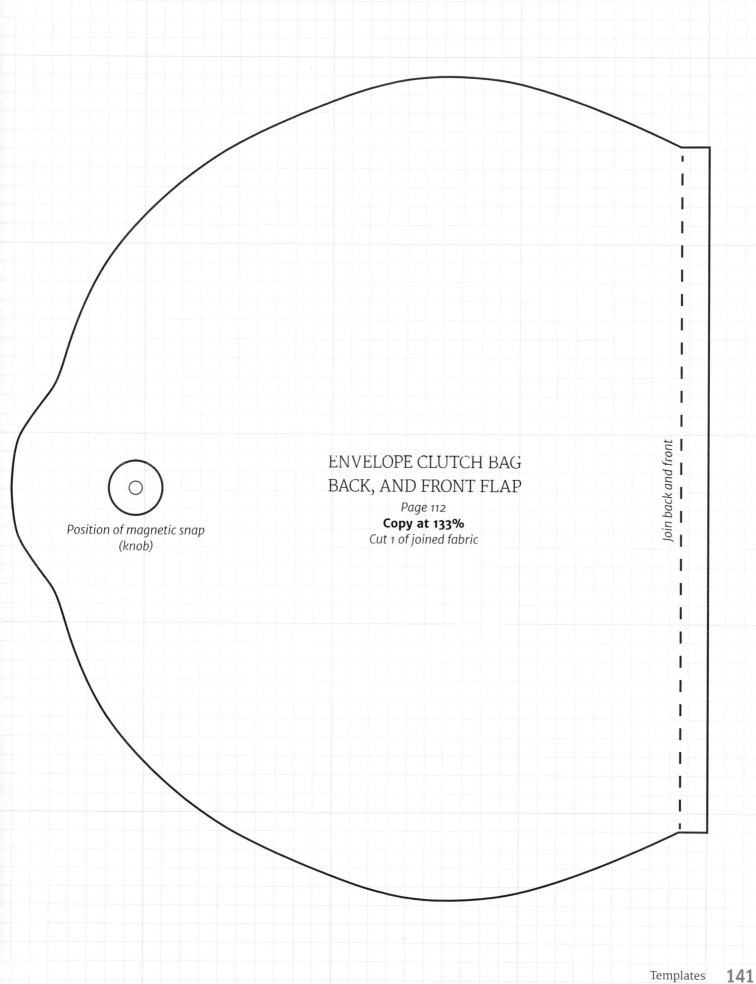

Position of magnetic snap
(knob)

ENVELOPE CLUTCH BAG
BACK, AND FRONT FLAP
Page 112
Copy at 133%
Cut 1 of joined fabric

Join back and front

RESOURCES

Cotton fabrics, fat quarters
www.cottonpatch.co.uk
www.craftcotton.com
www.fabricland.co.uk

Ripstop nylon, waterproof fabrics
www.ukfabricsonline.com

Embroidery threads
www.cloudcraft.co.uk

Sewing machines & accessories
www.jaycotts.co.uk

General haberdashery
www.sewandsew.co.uk

Zips & fastenings, basting tape
www.sewessential.co.uk

Fusible interfacing, fleece & foam
www.empressmills.co.uk

Bag fastenings & clasps
www.u-handbag.com

ACKNOWLEDGEMENTS

Many thanks to Jonathan Bailey for asking me to write this book,
to Sara Harper for her patience and organizational skills, to Cath Senker
for editing the text so meticulously, Neal Grundy for photographing the
finished bags and purses, and Wayne Blades for styling the projects and
designing such attractive pages. Thanks also to my Mum for teaching
me to sew in the first place, and to my daughters Lillie and Edith
for their advice and input.

INDEX

To order a book, or to request
a catalogue, contact:

GMC Publications Ltd
Castle Place, 166 High Street,
Lewes, East Sussex,
BN7 1XU
United Kingdom
Tel: +44 (0)1273 488005
www.gmcbooks.com